THE
ELEPHANT
IN THE
ROOM

CHURCH SCHOOLS ARE DROWNING—
CHAMPIONS NEEDED!

SADRAIL SAINT-ULYSSE, PhD, MDiv

ISBN 978-1-63961-783-8 (paperback)
ISBN 978-1-63961-784-5 (digital)

Christian Faith Publishing, Inc.
832 Park Avenue
Meadville, PA 16335
www.christianfaithpublishing.com

Printed in the United States of America

To the memories of my parents, Eglantine and Saint-Hilaire, who never experienced a formal education

To my siblings, especially my eldest sister, Aida, who introduced me to the Seventh-day Adventist faith and education at a very young age

To my lovely wife, Malou, who inspired me to join the Adventist school system as an educator

To my son, Sadou, who challenges me with his bright and inquisitive mind

Finally, to the memory of Dr. Edna I. E. Hunter, for being a champion to church schools at the Collingwood Park Seventh-day Adventist Church and Meadow View Junior Academy

*These commandments that I give you today
are to be on your hearts. Impress them on
your children. Talk about them when you sit
at home and when you walk along the road,
when you lie down and when you get up.
Tie them as symbols on your hands and bind
them on your foreheads. Write them on the
doorframes of your houses and on your gates.*

—Deuteronomy 6:6–9 (NIV)

CONTENTS

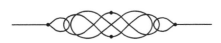

FOREWORD

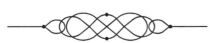

I first met Dr. Sadrail Saint-Ulysse in 2015 as a Christian Education growth coach who teaches marketing as an intentional ministry. With our first encounter, there was an immediate attraction of like-mindedness with a singular purpose of making Christian education better and accessible to all families.

In this book, Sadrail takes you into his world—a place of Christ-driven honesty, transparency, grace, passion, history, humility, and most importantly bravery! At his core, Sadrail is a courageous leader who is not afraid of 'the elephant in the room' and 'can get into some good trouble' concerning the challenges that impact Christian education.

In my coaching practice, working with hundreds of Christian schools across the nation, I have found that successful outcomes in Christian education happen while working together in a community that includes the home, church, and school.

This book will help you embrace the inculcation power of the triple-braided cord of home, church, and school. In Ecclesiastes 4:12, the Bible tells us that "though one may be overpowered, two can defend themselves. A cord of three strands is not quickly broken." Can a child with the home, church and school form the foundations for a Christian life separately or bound together?

Let's do some math to find out!

Time spent at church engaging our children averages out to be approximately 2-4 hours a week. The arithmetic accounts for 1 hour for the church service; 1 hour of Bible study and up to 2 additional hours if involved in church activities like Pathfinders or Adventurers. The final calculation shows that some children will only get 1 hour (attend church service only), some 2 hours (church and Bible study), and some more if they participate in other available church activities. Is 2-4 hours each week enough time to equip our children for a secular world and a life-long walk with Jesus Christ?

Next, let's account for time spent at home. According to the 2019 U.S. Bureau of Labor Statistics, a parent with children under the age of 18 will spend about an average of 1.36 hours per day caring for and helping household children. This data includes physical care, reading, playing (not sports), and activities related to education. Is an average of fewer than 10 hours a week at home enough time to equip our children for a secular world and a life-long walk with Jesus Christ?

And lastly, depending on state requirements as recorded in the National Center for Educational Statistics, children spend an average of 7 hours a day for approximately 180 days of instruction each year in public school. This does not include any before or after-school activities; excluding weekends and holidays. The school hours and days are similar for Christian schools. Is 35 or more hours each week at school enough to expose (public school) or equip (Christian school) our children for a secular world and a life-long walk with Jesus Christ?

Draw your conclusion on which portion of the cord is the strongest. If braided together, can the cord be even stronger?

You will learn in this book that Christian schools are in urgent need of many things:

- Engaged churches and pastors
- Action school boards

- Dedicated teachers
- Parents as partners
- Community collaboration
- Unification of the ministry of church and school along with funding for students and facilities.

Along the way, you will begin to understand why systemic change can reap a significant return on investment for those who champion!

As members of a triple-braided community, we can become purposeful 'champions.' Personified, we are helping 'champions', praying 'champions', loving 'champions', cooking 'champions', clean-up 'champions', fundraising 'champions', willingness-of-spirit 'champions', and so on.

It is critical to stop and think about what kinds of 'champions' we want and what kind of 'champions' we don't. We don't want 'champions' that are negative. We don't wish for accusing 'champions', gossiping 'champions', or demanding 'champions.' We do want 'champions' that say-I can help, 'champions' that applaud, and check writing 'champions'! We do want 'champions' that are positive cheerleaders and 'champions' that never discourage!

'Champions' are stay-at-home and working moms and dads, uncles and aunts, grandparents, pastors, board members, donors, and friends who care passionately about children and Christian education. It is you and I, as 'champions' that make the difference.

Becoming a 'champion' does not mean a huge time commitment. Any gift of time or talent makes a more considerable difference than you can imagine. Becoming a 'champion' can give you great joy! Each school has tasks to fit every schedule and interest. There are even tasks that do not involve coming to the school at all and can be accomplished from home.

So what are we to do? This question forms the strategy for what lies ahead in making Christian education better and accessible to all families. Sadrail and I both know firsthand the transformative power of champions!

Enjoy the read. Embrace the challenge. Be a Champion! Go with God!

Teresa L. Kelchner
Christian Education Champion, Advocate, and Coach.
President, www.ChristianEducationMatters.com
Co-Founder, www.MinistrySpotlight.com
Founder, www.ChampionsForChristianEducation.com

PREFACE

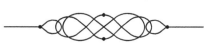

As I wrote and did research for this book, I almost concluded that this book was not needed because of the excellent materials produced by the brilliant minds of the Seventh-day Adventist Church worldwide. These materials are readily available on the Internet in several websites such as *The Journal of Adventist Education, Circle, and Ministry*, to name a few. I decided to go ahead with this project because while there are all these valuable resources, they are written in the form of articles and reports that are not too often searched for by our teachers, principals, pastors, administrators, and church members.

I borrowed from the work of these brilliant authors of our Church and added my humble and candid voice in this book. I did a lot of rewriting so as not to offend any individual or entity while at the same time addressing the issue at hand. It was not an easy undertaking. However, I praise God for the opportunity to write this book, with the prayer that it may help bring and keep more students in our church schools at the elementary and secondary levels.

Furthermore, as an educator and pastor, as I looked for practical and valuable resources in the forms of books, I found very few to name; I only found two: *How to Kill Adventist Education (and How to Give It a Fighting Chance)* (2009) and *Peril and Promise: Adventist Education at the Crossroads* (2012). These two books have helped me tremendously in my ministry as a superintendent of schools, and I pray that this book may be a blessing to some. My prayer is that the number of elementary and secondary church schools that we currently have in the North American Division and especially in the New Jersey Conference and Columbia Union, where I have been serving since 1998, and throughout the world Church, may grow and not be diminished as we await the soon return of our Lord and Savior, Jesus Christ. Maranatha!

ACKNOWLEDGMENTS

The views expressed in this book are mine. I owe a great debt of gratitude to the brilliant minds of the Seventh-day Adventist educators and friends for their contribution to *The Journal of Adventist Education* and other sources. In writing this book, I turned to their great work on behalf of Adventist education. Also, special thanks to my colleagues and friends who were selected to review the first manuscripts. I will not name them because I am fully responsible for the good and especially the bad in this book. Thank you!

I thank the New Jersey Conference administrators, especially presidents, whom I have worked with from 1998 through today. Each one has helped shape my thinking and standing for Adventist education. I also thank the teachers, principals, school administrators and staff, pastors, board members, church members, and elders whom I have worked with to benefit our precious students in the New Jersey Conference.

Furthermore, a special thank-you to Meadow View Junior Academy (MVJA), its district and constituent churches, and Collingwood Park SDA Church and The Grace Place SDA Church for their prayers and support in working with my wife and me to try many ideas and programs to promote, support, and making it a reality for MVJA to be a school where every student can be enrolled and remained regardless of his or her family's financial ability. Great will be your rewards in heaven. Thank you!

Finally, my heartfelt gratitude to Dr. A Kay Schaaf for her editing assistance. She has encouraged me to rewrite my manuscript to include the wider Christian Church, for which I am grateful. My family and I praise God for Dr. Kay's friendship and encouragement through the years.

To the entire team of Christian Faith Publishing for helping me make this book a reality. I praise God for using Christian Faith Publishing to help me with this book.

INTRODUCTION

TIME TO GET INTO *GOOD TROUBLE* FOR CHURCH SCHOOLS

*"For I know the plans I have for you," declares
the Lord, "plans to prosper you and not to harm
you, plans to give you hope and a future."*
—Jeremiah 29:11 (NIV)

The *New York Times* published an essay written by Congressman John Lewis, the civil rights leader, on the day of his funeral. Congressman Lewis penned the following words shortly before his death: "Though I am gone, I urge you to answer the highest calling of your heart and stand up for what you truly believe."[1] I am standing for church schools, Adventist education in particular at the elementary and secondary levels, since I am a Seventh-day Adventist educator and pastor. I also call on Christian church members to do the same by standing for Christian education in their denominations locally and worldwide.

In his essay, Congressman Lewis calls on "ordinary people with extraordinary vision" to get in what he calls "good trouble, necessary trouble." I am standing as an ordinary person with extraordinary vision for Christian education, Adventist elementary and secondary schools in particular, in the United States and worldwide, knowing that I may get in trouble, good trouble, for something I believe in—church schools. I can't remain silent any longer. Before COVID, many Christian schools, including Adventist schools, were struggling and even dying. During this pandemic and post-pandemic, unless we call for and make systemic changes at every local church or parish level to the highest level of church leadership or religious leadership, I cannot imagine the worst. For instance, in a recent article dated May 10, 2021, published by the *Wall Street Journal*, entitled "Catholic Schools Are Losing Students at Record Rates, and Hundreds Are Closing," Lovett stated the following:

> At least 209 of the country's nearly 6,000 Catholic schools have closed over the past year, according to the National Catholic Educational Association. More closures are expected this summer, and some schools have taken to GoFundMe in an effort to stay open.
>
> Nationwide, Catholic school enrollment fell 6.4% at the start of this school year, the largest single-year decline since the NCEA began tracking such data in the 1970s.
>
> Urban dioceses have been hit especially hard: Enrollment in schools run by the Catholic Archdiocese of Los Angeles was down 12% at the start of this school year. In the Archdiocese of New York, enrollment was down 11%.[2]

I also looked up the most recent statistics for Adventist elementary and secondary schools in the United States and Canada, known as the North American Division. According to the website of the Education department of the North American Division, elementary school enrollment fell by 10.93% from 38,182 students in the 2019–2020 school year to 34,007 students for the 2020–2021 school year. Similarly, there was an 8.62% decrease in student enrollment at the secondary level from 12,135 students in the 2019–2020 school year to 11,089 students in the 2020–2021 school year. The same website indicated a 2.22% of school closure during the 2020–2021 school year among PK–10 grade schools.[3] Enrollment in Adventist schools in the North American Division was fairly constant before the pandemic. However, the statistics cited above have demonstrated the fragility of Christian schools' enrollment.

To surmount the devastating consequence of the pandemic, each religious organization, beginning at the local level to the highest level, must rethink and change its policies on financing Christian elementary and secondary schools to bring much needed life to an already struggling school system. I humbly tackle this book project to shed light to this problem as I reflect on my own journey involving in elementary and secondary church schools in the hope to bring possible solutions for consideration. As I address this issue, I am reminded of a recent conversation with a few colleagues. We were addressing the challenges of financing church schools, Adventist schools, in particular. One of my colleagues stated that there are those based on their positions in the local church or at different levels of the church organization who have influence to drive change and those with the power to bring about these changes. Some have the influence to bring about issues that may someday make it to the agenda. There are others who not only have the power to propose—or better yet, dictate—what should be on the agenda, have also the power to support and ensure that these items translate into action. I appeal to each one to use his or her influence and power to benefit our precious children regardless of their families' financial standing to give them access to Christian education as commanded by Jesus in the Great Commission (Matthew 28:18–20). The Christian Church, regardless of the denomination, must not neglect its own children and youth as it seeks to evangelize the world. Evangelism must begin with our children. The best way to evangelize our children and youth in partnership with the home and church is through and by our Christian schools.

Please don't think of me as a brave one who dares to go where many have not gone before. I am not. I do not consider myself brave. I don't usually look for trouble—although trouble has found me—most of the time. I prayed hard about putting this book together. I also did a lot of research because many have spoken on this topic.

Thankfully, I have found many brilliant minds in the Adventist Church who spoke of the challenges of financing church schools and how they might be addressed. I plan to use their work, their voices, and make my own noise for our church schools, elementary, and secondary schools.

I pray that this book will bring church members, pastors, parents, local church leaders, board members, and leaders at all levels of the Church to do something about it. To make systemic and sustainable changes for our children, we need real action—no more words or bandages. We need systemic changes. We need policy changes at every level of the Church to ensure that every Christian family with elementary and secondary school-age children can enroll and remain in Christian schools, regardless of his or her financial standing. Budgetary changes at every level to assist Christian elementary and secondary schools are necessary during these turbulent times.

The Lord has blessed the Christian Church with brilliant minds. Most, if not all these educators, have been a part of our Church school system whether at the elementary, secondary, or tertiary levels. They have given eloquent speeches and have written brilliant articles, but nothing has changed. The policies that have plagued our schools remain. No real change that I can see at my level as a superintendent of schools and pastor in the Seventh-day Adventist Church.

In this book, I plan to stand on the shoulders of several Christian authors, mostly Adventist authors, who have addressed the challenges that Christian schools, church schools, have faced. However, local churches and leadership at the regional, national, and global levels have not made any policy changes to resolve these challenges. I am now adding my voice, my perspective, in a not-so-subtle fashion, as an immigrant and practitioner, superintendent of schools in the Adventist school system, who is married to a teaching principal to appeal to the Christian Church at every level to do something.

I write this book as a concerned superintendent of schools and church pastor who is married to a church school principal and has experienced firsthand the burden of financing church schools even before the pandemic. Financing church schools became heavier during the pandemic. Seeing firsthand the toll on my wife as she navigates her added responsibilities as a frontline and essential worker, I remember a childhood friend whose parents were workers of the Seventh-day Adventist Church. My friend's father served as a pastor and her mother as an educator. My friend commented to me that she would never marry a pastor. She felt that the work of the church caused her mother's untimely death, as she [her mother] had to take on the responsibility of operating the schools of the churches where her father was assigned. As I watched my wife and spoke to other principals, I understood better my friend.

Will I get in trouble? Hopefully, *good trouble* so that we can finally make positive changes at the local church, regional, national, and global levels to benefit God's precious children, our elementary and secondary school-age students, here in the United States of America and around the world. Anything for God's cause. Anything for the most valuable part of our Church, his Church, our children, his children.

CHAPTER 1

MY JOURNEY IN CHURCH SCHOOLS

Can a mother forget the baby at her breast and
have no compassion on the child she has borne?
Though she may forget, I will not forget you!
— Isaiah 49:15 (NIV)

For nearly twenty-five years, I have served as a chaplain, teacher, vice-principal, principal, and now superintendent of schools in the same conference, the New Jersey Conference of Seventh-day Adventists. I was introduced to church schools by my eldest sister, Aida, when she became a Seventh-day Adventist in Haiti. I was seven years old when she introduced my eight siblings and me to the Adventist faith and education. At the time, there were two Adventist schools in Port-au-Prince, Haiti. Three of my siblings and I were enrolled in the Adventist school near our home, Ecole Adventiste de Vertières, now Collège Vertières, the elementary school located next to Eben Ezer, the church where I was later baptized.

Ecole Adventiste de Vertières was a multi-grade school at the time. I learned and did very well. My education was not inferior to any others. I recently called my eldest sister, Aida, who enrolled my siblings and me in the Seventh-day Adventist elementary church school. I asked her why she decided that it was the school for me and my siblings when she became Seventh-day Adventist. I was hoping that she would say that she was encouraged to do so by her pastor, elders, or the church members, and wishing she was told that it was the best way to bring us up as Seventh-day Adventists. I was hoping that she would tell me that she was taught as a new member in the Seventh-day Adventist Church that "the work of education and the work of redemption are one"[1] as God inspired the footprints for education to one of our founders, Ellen G. White. My sister simply told me that the Seventh-day Adventist education system was known to be among the best in Haiti. She chose it for us because it was the best. There were many other private schools in Port-au-Prince, Haiti, at that time.

How glad I am that my sister chose an Adventist school for me as I entered first grade. I had a great experience as a child attending that church school as an elementary student. I loved seeing my teachers on Sabbaths. I loved even seeing some of my classmates who attended that church on Sabbaths. I said "some of my classmates" because it was the only Seventh-day Adventist school in that area serving several large churches. The enrollment was such that the school was a multi-grade school; I can't recall how many there were of us in the first and second grades classroom.

My years at Ecole Adventiste de Vertières were short-lived. Soon after my enrollment, my sister emigrated to the United States to help our family gain a better life. My parents, who were farmers, sold some of their properties to send her to the United States. She encountered a lot of challenges and could not send us the funds needed to pay for our tuition. I was sent home and spent part of my elementary education homeschooled by my older siblings before continuing at another private school.

Upon entering the United States in twelfth grade, I continued my education at a public school. After completing an associate degree in medical technology and a bachelor's degree in biology, I decided to follow God's calling for my life to become a Seventh-day Adventist pastor by enrolling at Andrews University Theological Seminary, where I earned a Master of Divinity degree. After I graduated from Andrews University, my wife and I joined Garden State Academy in 1998; myself as chaplain and my wife taught also. After completing a second master's degree in Educational Administration with an emphasis in K–12 at Centenary University, I later re-enrolled at Andrews University to complete a PhD in educational administration with an emphasis in higher education.

CHAPTER 2

APPEALING FOR SYSTEMIC CHANGE

Have I not commanded you? Be strong
and courageous. Do not be afraid; do not
be discouraged, for the Lord your God
will be with you wherever you go.
—Joshua 1:9

Throughout this book, I appeal for systemic change in the Seventh-day Adventist Church to help resolve the challenge of financing Seventh-day Adventist education at the elementary and secondary levels. I also appeal to other Christian denominations to do the same to help resolve the challenges in their church schools. Changes, while necessary, are not usually welcomed. A quote attributed to Albert Einstein states, "Problems cannot be solved by the same level of thinking that created them."[1] I am calling or appealing for systemic change in the Seventh-day Adventist Church to address a problem that has existed since the time of our pioneer, Ellen White, financing Adventist education. Adventist education appears to have been secondary to the mission of the Adventist Church, although Ellen White has stated, "in the highest sense the work of education and the work of redemption are one."[2]

While the Seventh-day Adventist Church has spent a considerable amount of money in elementary and secondary schools, historically, the Adventist Church *has not* supported its elementary and secondary schools at the level that they need to be financially sustainable. So I write this book to do something that most would consider unwise as a current employee of the Seventh-day Adventist Church. I call or appeal for systemic change—change in policies that have kept the financial support from tithe and other sources to Adventist elementary and secondary schools at minimal. I also challenge other fellow Christian believers to prioritize Christian elementary and secondary schools as a necessary ministry that should not be neglected. We must educate our children and youth in the ways of the Lord. Our children must be taught of the Lord (Isaiah 54:13), and our Christian schools are necessary to make this a reality.

I am calling for systemic change at every level of the Church, vertically and horizontally.[3] Vertical changes which involve changes in existing policies for financing education at the local, regional, national, and global levels. Horizontal changes which involve the local church (church members, church leaders, parents, and pastors or other religious leaders) and elementary and secondary school levels (church boards, principals, teachers, and school staff). This is not a book about finger-pointing. Everyone at every level must do his/her part to bring about these positive changes to benefit our precious children and young people.

Systemic change means a fundamental change[4] to ensure that every Seventh-day Adventist elementary and secondary age child can attend his or her church schools regardless of his or her families' ability to pay the school tuition. Systemic change so that every Christian child can attend his or her church school regardless of his or her family's financial status. An analysis of the rationale for *the call* or appeal for systemic change can be explained as follows: "All systems organize individual pieces into some sort of interrelated whole. Put simply, systemic change occurs when change reaches all or most parts of a system, thus affecting the general behavior of the entire system. However, systemic change is often difficult to envision, let alone encourage, because people generally find it easier to focus on the parts than on the systems that connect those pieces."[5] Each one must see the necessity and make it a priority to educate our children in our church schools. Every Christian child deserves a Christian education. It is the duty of every Christian church member to make it a reality.

Local church and school boards often complain about how leadership at the district, state, regional, and national levels are not giving enough financial support to Christian elementary and secondary schools. At the district and regional levels, one may hear how there is not enough financial support at the national and global levels. To bring systemic change at every level we must ask ourselves what we are doing or not doing to help the schools financially, and at the same time, engage others to do what is necessary to address the financial crisis in elementary and secondary schools, especially in churches, districts, and states that are composed primarily of immigrants and where government aids or school vouchers are not available. This book seeks to bring about the discussion and resolve on financing Christian schools or church schools at every level of the Church from the local church, district and state-level leadership, regional, national, and global-level leadership to bring about systemic change to make Christian elementary and secondary schools affordable to the children of the members of the Church.

CHAPTER 3

MY BITTERSWEET EXPERIENCE

I know of but one way: find a field of
labor, ask God to help, take off your
coat, and pitch into the work.
                                        —J. N. Andrews

The above quote is one of my favorite quotes from J. N. Andrews, known as the first official Seventh-day Adventist missionary. Andrews University, my alma mater at the master's and doctoral levels, is named after this great Seventh-day Adventist pioneer. My wife, Malou, and I have found that *field of labor* to be in Church schools both elementary and secondary schools, and especially in the State of New Jersey since 1998. It is a rather interesting story.

In the early to mid-'70s, my eldest sister, Aida, whom I referenced earlier in this book, and my wife's mother, Theresena, emigrated to the United States, and both landed in New Jersey. Why the great state of New Jersey? Only God knows, but New Jersey has become what my wife and I call "our little Haiti." If you find us in any states outside of New Jersey and you ask us where we are from, we will quickly say "New Jersey." We have learned to be careful through the years with the many unusual looks or sometimes unwelcomed comments that my wife and I have received, even within the Seventh-day Adventist Church circle. We are two individuals who love New Jersey and have called New Jersey home even with our non-New Jersey native accent.

My wife and I have made the New Jersey Conference our home since we arrived in the United States. I was seventeen years old when I first came to New Jersey—shall I say, not too long ago? Time has passed by too quickly. My wife, Malou, was fourteen. New Jersey is where we came after landing at John F. Kennedy International Airport in New York. My sister and Malou's mother had been living in New Jersey for several years when we arrived. They both shared the same pastor in two different churches. While Malou and I also shared the same mathematics teacher in two different private schools in Haiti, we did not meet in Haiti. As we retraced our paths, we must have crossed paths in Port-au-Prince. Since I am five years older than she is (or used to be), I often joked that she would have been too young for me to notice her at that time. This subject is for another book. New Jersey became our home, a welcoming place; a place where many immigrants who look like me reside. A place where many immigrants have been welcomed before and after us as inscribed in the Statue of Liberty:

> Give me your tired, your poor,
> Your huddled masses yearning to breathe free,
> The wretched refuse of your teeming shore.
> Send these, the homeless, tempest-tost to me,
> I lift my lamp beside the golden door![1]

I came to find refuge in the United States, in New Jersey in particular, when I joined my sister Aida and her family. As a new immigrant, I attended and graduated from the public high school, Vailsburg High School, in Newark. Malou attended a public school in Jersey City, where she spent her first four years before moving to Massachusetts to attend Atlantic Union College.

After I graduated from Jersey City State College, now New Jersey City University, and Malou from Atlantic Union College—both with degrees in biology—we got married and moved to Andrews University, Michigan, on the same day of our wedding. We spent our first three years of marriage learning and preparing for *our field of labor*, Adventist education in New Jersey. Malou and I knew that we wanted to serve in New Jersey. When we enrolled at Andrews University, I at the seminary and Malou at the school of business, we knew that we would return to New Jersey to serve, primarily the Haitian Americans, whom we have become part of and very much related to. At the seminary, I first learned the terminology of being sponsored by a conference. I attempted a sponsorship from the New Jersey Conference while at the seminary, which was not successful. So we both worked as student workers on campus and added additional student loans to complete our masters' degrees.

We returned to New Jersey to our friends and families, and with the blessing of the New Jersey Conference (without financial support), planted All Nations Community SDA Church. Our church plant started with a group of our families and friends. We called it a church from the very beginning because people come to church, not to group. While at Andrews University, my wife and I attended as many church planting seminars as we could because we knew that we would be planting a church for a group of people who have adopted the American way of life while remaining Haitians at heart. Sometimes this is very hard to explain or comprehend.

As we returned to New Jersey in the summer of 1998, we quickly learned of an opening at Garden State Academy (GSA), a place that my wife and I recalled with fond memories. The campus was not new to us. We had been there at several camp meetings and Pathfinder events. We never thought that we would one day live and work there or even begin our ministry and family there. Our son, Sadou, was born two years after we moved back to New Jersey. It became his and our very special place. We have made great friends at GSA, students and colleagues, who will be in our hearts throughout eternity. My wife first joined as a full-time teacher and I as a Bible teacher and chaplain. While I enjoyed my new calling, I quickly learned that I could not keep the new church planting and my assignments at the academy. We remained in touch with the church as we joined them every school break. We loved our GSA family and experience. I was ordained as a minister while working at GSA. It did not take us long to discover that we had joined an academy that had been experiencing financial challenges through the years.

Garden State Academy had changed as the conference demographics had also changed. When I first joined the New Jersey Conference as a new immigrant in 1983, it was mostly a Caucasian conference. I do not have the statistics for that time, but now the New Jersey Conference is mostly an immigrant conference with statistics surpassing that of the North American Division (NAD) of Seventh-day Adventists and the state of New Jersey in terms of immigrants. It is reported that "nearly a third of the members in the North American Division (31 percent) were not born as citizens of their current nation of residence, Bermuda, Canada, or the US. This percentage represents an immigration rate nearly three times the national rate in the US and Canada."[2] In a document published by American Immigration Council (2020), it is noted that in the state of New Jersey, "nearly one-quarter of the state's population was born in another country, while one in six residents is a native-born US citizen with at least one immigrant parent."[3] The New Jersey Conference membership is comprised of about 60 percent of first-generation immigrants, with mostly individuals from Spanish-speaking countries.

I love being part of a conference filled with immigrants, mostly new immigrants like me. My family feels at home in New Jersey. We don't have to drive too far to shop at international grocery stores or worship at a non-English-speaking church. We love New Jersey. We love the New Jersey Conference of Seventh-day Adventists.

While my wife and I enjoy serving in a place with many new immigrants, it does come with many financial challenges. Garden State Academy had changed to now representing the New Jersey Conference demographics, as stated earlier, with students mostly from new immigrant families, from New York City, primarily minorities. Needless to say, that recent immigrants have not yet accumulated wealth in the new land, and many struggle immensely to make ends meet. The American Immigration Council (2020) cited earlier noted that "most immigrants in New Jersey have pursued education at or above the college level."[4] Furthermore, "two in five (40 percent) adult immigrants had a college degree or more education in 2018, while just under one in five (18 percent) had less than a high school diploma."[5] I am sure that many immigrants with college degrees carry large amount of debt in school loans. I am not aware of the educational statistics within the New Jersey Conference.

Garden State Academy, like many other academies near large cities, offered not only a safe Christian family atmosphere for students to be not only educated to make a difference in their world as they prepare for college, but mostly to meet and fall in love with Jesus as they await his soon coming. Many students' lives were changed at GSA. While we had students from families from all walks of life, we were seen by many for being a school of inner-city youth because of the high percentage of minority students enrolled. The school suffered greatly as many chose other academies with fewer minority students for their children. The academy became a financial burden rather than a ministry. In 2005, seven years after we joined Garden State Academy, the doors closed, or shall I say, "ceased to operate," the term used in official votes in committees to close the academy.

While at Garden State Academy, I embraced the quotation cited earlier from J. N. Andrews: "I know of but one way: find a field of labor, ask God to help, take off your coat, and pitch into the work." My wife and I, along with our colleagues at GSA, worked very hard to keep the academy running. We sacrificed pay raises and worked many long hours. I became a recruiter while teaching and serving as one of the vice-principals. I even embarked on a fundraising effort trying to raise the needed funds to keep the academy in operation for just one more year. I remember sending a letter to the alumni and other educators and church leaders asking for financial support. Some believed that the academy would never close because it was God's school. We received more prayers than financial support to raise the needed funds. Our son, Sadou, was four years old at the time. He started collecting pennies and quarters around the house to help us keep the academy open. Our hearts were broken when we finally realized that our efforts could not keep the school open. We prayed and cried and looked for a new "field of labor," hopefully in New Jersey, to serve.

CHAPTER 4

A NEW OPPORTUNITY TO SERVE

See, I am doing a new thing! Now it springs up;
do you not perceive it? I am making a way in
the wilderness and streams in the wasteland.
                              —Isaiah 43:19 (NIV)

With the help of the Good Lord, my wife and I received a new assignment to continue to serve within the New Jersey Conference at another school in central Jersey, Meadow View Junior Academy (MVJA), myself as a principal/teacher and Malou as a teacher. I was well-prepared to serve as a principal because during my seven years in education at Garden State Academy (GSA), I completed a second master's degree in Educational Administration at Centenary College, now Centenary University in Hackettstown, New Jersey. While at GSA, I also completed a certification in Information Technology at Seaton Hall University in South Orange, New Jersey.

At Meadow View Junior Academy (MVJA), we were welcomed by a new school family. While we missed the boarding academy experience and our high school students/friends, we welcomed the new experience and the challenges. I quickly realized that being a full-time teacher and principal of a junior academy was as time consuming as working at a boarding school, if not more. The days were long, if not longer, but we were once again working together as a family. My wife returned to work teaching elementary grades 6 through 8 and I teaching grades 9 and 10 and our son in kindergarten. Sadou enjoyed the experience as an only child. Now he could see more students of his age. He admired what he called "large families" and wished that he had other siblings. I jokingly reminded him that we could not afford more children because we both had to work and had student loans to pay. My wife stayed at home and taught a class or two while we were at the academy. During that time, she completed her elementary teaching certificate. Now it was time for both of us to work and take care of our student loans, a large amount of money owed while attending Adventist higher education—the subject for another book.

Our family enjoyed visiting the churches in our new community. We have found many churches and members who believe and supported Meadow View Junior Academy through the years. We started to make new friends and quickly learned the difference between teaching at a boarding school and a day school. The transition to a junior academy was seamless. We had a great community of parents and grandparents. At the time that we joined MVJA, the school had a mixture of races. The school quickly changed to a mostly Black and Hispanic student body as the demography of the churches in the community also changed. The New Jersey Conference continued to grow but mostly with immigrants joining the churches.

My wife and I continued to be involved in recruiting and added fundraising to our portfolio, knowing that the financial needs were real. We have worked with a great board there, and the school nearly doubled its original enrollment by the time I left to join the New Jersey Conference as superintendent of schools. Since I was an ordained pastor serving as a principal and teacher as part of my new assignment as the superintendent of schools, I was given a church to pastor; another new opportunity to serve.

CHAPTER 5

A PRINCIPAL AND TEACHER: LESSONS LEARNED

Love the Lord your God with all your heart and
with all your soul and with all your strength.
These commandments that I give you today
are to be on your hearts. Impress them on
your children. Talk about them when you sit
at home and when you walk along the road,
when you lie down and when you get up.
—Deuteronomy 6:5–7 (NIV)

From my perspective as a principal of a Christian school, the work of the principal and teacher is a humble one. I have learned to apologize even before I understand what my mistakes were; there are not enough hours in the day (nor in the night, if there is such an expression). I usually joke with my family that English is my third language, and I also can create my own expressions in the English language having lived in America for so long and having earned a PhD in the Unites States. I needed to learn about humility so that the Lord afforded me the blessing of being a principal/teacher.

From the time I joined Garden State Academy in 1998, I knew that I wanted to be a principal. I have always been a leader. I was raised in a family where I was allowed to be myself, and at times,

34

lead even as the baby of the family. I was often told of my leadership abilities by my family and friends, and later, by my wife who believes that I am one of the greatest leaders. It is good to be loved.

As a child growing up in Haiti where soccer was the prominent or only sport of that time, I was engaged in soccer every summer. In Haiti, the school days were spent in school activities. There was no time for any other activities. Even during the summer months, my parents paid money for us to be tutored. However, we were allowed to play soccer, lots of it, during the summer. I soon learned that soccer was not for me. I decided to become the leader of the team and raised funds for our uniforms and soccer balls, which needed to be changed very often in Desdunes, the town/province where I spent most of my summers as a child.

I was in a better position than most principals in the Seventh-day Adventist school system because I became a principal after seven years of teaching and four years as a vice-principal. During those seven years, I worked with three great principals and learned a lot from each one of them. As I worked as a principal, I came to appreciate them even more. I quickly learned that it takes a team, which I prefer to use the word *family*, to make a great school. While every school needs a strong educational leader, it takes an entire community to have a great school. During my four years working as a principal/teacher, I was blessed working with two very supportive school board chairs. I knew that they both loved and supported the school very much.

I believe that our church schools are necessary to the spiritual, mental, physical, and social development of our children. Meadow View Junior Academy was a multi-grade school. I quickly learned the challenge of recruiting students to church schools from the churches because the school was a multi-grade school. I came to appreciate my teaching principal when I attended a Seventh-day Adventist elementary school in Haiti. Promoting the Adventist curriculum and school program was not a challenge. Our Adventist school curriculum meets and even surpasses national and state standards. Since our son was a student at Meadow View Junior Academy, parents could see that we trusted the Adventist school system with the education of our one and only child's education.

While my wife and I selected a church family in the Meadow View Junior Academy community, we visited all the churches in our school community. We had to pass on the many invitations for Sabbath lunches at the churches and friendly members' homes. We enjoyed visiting the churches and looking for new families for our school. Soon many families started to literally run away from me after the church service because they knew that I would speak with them about enrolling their child or children at our great Seventh-day Adventist school, MVJA. My wife helped me a lot with her love for languages when visiting Spanish-speaking churches. I believed that our school was for every student regardless of their cultural backgrounds or financial ability to pay.

I found it also difficult to recruit non-Seventh-day Adventist students. Some families from the community joined our preschool with the understanding that they would leave once their children were ready to start kindergarten or first grade. We had a family who shared with us the love for our school. However, the father commented that he could not continue to pay for his child's education beyond kindergarten. Furthermore, he stated that the public school also offered him the opportunity to interact with his neighbors whose children attend the same public school. Later, Meadow View Junior Academy had to close the preschool when the public school started to offer preschool and a full-day kindergarten program.

I also learned very quickly as a principal the importance of having supportive pastors, and I was blessed with several. I quickly learned that once you have a supportive pastor, the entire church will follow suit with students and funding for the school. One of the pastors who was a great believer and supporter of church schools told me upon my being hired at MVJA that the lack of money would not stop any student at his church from attending the school. The tuition for every child whose family was a member of his church was fully paid. My wife and I missed him after he left that church to be a pastor in another state. I am sure that he continues to be a blessing to that school community. He attended Seventh-day Adventist schools through the college level and believed in the mission of Seventh-day Adventist education. We need more pastors who understand and support the mission of our church schools.

I usually joke that I have only met one principal who was better at recruiting than me. The principal did something that I never thought of doing. The principal occasionally attended other Christian churches on Sundays to recruit students for the school. Although the principal really tried, he did not succeed at having any takers. The principal was a true evangelist not only to the Adventist community but also to the broader Christian community. It was very tiring, and at times discouraging, to recruit among the Seventh-day Adventist church members. One summer, I spent almost every Sunday on the phone calling every family with school age children. That summer, no new student enrolled. I only had one student who enrolled during the second semester. I learned to be humble as I was humbled, an experience that I shared later with principals as a superintendent. I shared this experience to encourage principals when after a long summer of recruiting did not see the results of their efforts.

I always tell principals that that recruiting for Christian schools is like the work of an evangelist at a church. You pray and preach your heart out. In the end, it is only the Holy Spirit who convicts the hearts and brings people to God. I never took the credit for a growing school. It is the work of the Holy Spirit touching the hearts of his children to do the right thing for their children. I was recently told of a great evangelist and pastor who told his church members that they should ask God for forgiveness for not enrolling their children at a Christian or church school. I have never put it this way, but there is a lot of truth to his statement. Moses in Deuteronomy 6 told the children of Israel how they should pass on their faith to their children. A text that I have used over and over in preaching and writing about church schools.

As a principal, I have learned to become an educational evangelist. I used the text in Deuteronomy 6 for many sermons and articles. I would do the following exercise during many sermons that I preached on Sabbaths. I would ask the members to look at the time, and then I ask, "Do you know where your child's teachers or principals were during the Sabbath day?" I would also emphasize the way that children learn. They learned through modeling. Teachers shared about their weekends to their students. I shared with my students how I spent my weekends; my Sabbaths experiences were very often shared with my students. I encouraged Seventh-day Adventist church members to choose a Seventh-day Adventist school for their children. I continue to do so as a superintendent of schools and pastor.

CHAPTER 6

MY SERVICE AS A SUPERINTENDENT

There can be no keener revelation of a society's
soul than the way in which it treats its children.
—Nelson Mandela, May 8, 1995

I received the call to serve as a superintendent of schools in 2009, four years after serving as a principal. The same year, 2009, the book *How to Kill Adventist Education and How to Give it a Fighting Chance*[1] by Pastor Shane Anderson was published. Not only did I read the book, I also bought copies for the principals, board chairs, and conference officers. I started with the objective to "give a fighting chance" to Adventist education. Anderson listed six primary factors, he believed, behind Adventist educational decline as follows:[2]

1. The lack of passion among churchgoing members for being a "conservative" Seventh-day Adventist.
2. A misunderstanding of what constitutes biblical discipleship.
3. Poor pastoral support of Adventist education.
4. Poor parenting.
5. The inroads of postmodernism, secularism, and "liberalism" in Adventism.
6. Poor-quality schools.

I set out to address these factors and help transform the Adventist schools in the New Jersey Conference. I took great notes reading the book because I had the opportunity to hear from the perspective of a pastor. I believed and continue to think that a lot of these factors were based from perceptions rather than reality. However, I was determined to address the areas that we needed to address so that when speaking of quality, we can articulate what it was. I started first by ensuring that every teacher in the New Jersey Conference had at least a bachelor's degree and held a denominational certification. Also, I ensured that principals completed their principal endorsement, which was not a requirement by the Columbia Union or the North American Division. Furthermore, I worked with every school board to ensure in addition to the denominational accreditation that every school in our conference received regional accreditation from Middle States Association Commissions on Elementary and Secondary Schools.

Additionally, we developed a program to bring more church support to the schools. Under this program, every church became part of a school district and was encouraged to support the school in its district by at least the equivalent of a student tuition which never came to fruition. We encouraged every school to adopt an electronic report card system. Again, perception matters.

These efforts were not easily accomplished, but the support of the division (the national level), union (the regional level), conference (the state level), principals, teachers, and boards helped to reach these goals. We worked collaboratively to enlarge our offerings by establishing a day academy with the possibility of more day academies in the future. We also embarked on plans to train and provide support to the schools in fundraising through the partnership with Philanthropic Service for Institutions (PSI). The work of the superintendent is very often misunderstood, but I feel blessed to work with like-minded colleagues to provide quality education to the children and youth in our conference. Our challenge continues to be with access to every Seventh-day Adventist child and youth due to the financial challenges of many families and churches. I believe other Christian denominations face the same financial challenge. The hurdle of funding can also be met with systemic changes.

The lack of funding for the schools caused by restrictive funding policies at churches, conferences, unions, divisions, and the General Conference levels can only be resolved by changing these policies to benefit our precious children and youth.

Like Pastor Anderson, I was reluctant to write on the topic of Adventist education, even as an insider. I am writing this book because I feel we need systemic changes so Adventist elementary and secondary schools everywhere can thrive during and post this pandemic. I write this book also to encourage other Christian denominations to do the same for their church schools. We cannot continue with business as usual. By addressing the issue of changes in policies as a Seventh-day Adventist Church employee, I may get in trouble, but I hope it will be *good trouble, necessary trouble* to bring about change by touching the hearts of parents, church members and leaders, conference leaders, union leaders, division leaders, executive committee members at every level, and the General Conference leaders.

While I write this book from the perspective of a member of the North American Division, I am certain other divisions, church members, and leaders, can also benefit from this book. Using statistics from the World Report 1991: Adventist Around the World, Dr. Humberto wrote an editorial for the *Journal of Adventist Education* entitled, "Global Trends in Adventist Education."[3] He stated that, educationally, our church is not keeping pace with its membership growth. Many Adventist parents are finding it more difficult to send their children to our schools.[4]

Dr. Humberto continued: From 1992 to 2018 the World Church membership grew from 7,498,653 members to 21,414,779,[5] 185.6% increase (Praise the Lord!). During that same period, student enrollment decreased by 23.5% (from 115 students per 1,000 members in 1992 to 88 students per 1,000 members). In 2018, student enrollment in the North American Division was about 60 students per 1,000 members,[6] which was about 32 percent lower when compared to the World Church. As cited above, our Seventh-day Adventist education system is not keeping pace with growth of the World Church, especially in North America. We, the local church, conference, union, division, and the General Conference, must do something about it.

CHAPTER 7

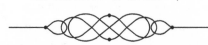

THE BIG DIVIDE: PASTORS AND SCHOOLS

*That all of them may be one, Father, just as you are
in me and I am in you. May they also be in us so
that the world may believe that you have sent me.*
—John 17:21 (NIV)

This is a challenging topic to address. One that may get me in trouble, indeed. As already stated, Anderson cited "poor pastoral support of Adventist education"[1] as one of the primary factors for the decline of Adventist schools. I am a pastor, and I am also a teacher. I attended the seminary to be trained to becoming a pastor, and my first assignment in the Adventist Church was that of a chaplain and Bible teacher. I also taught Algebra 1 because I was certified to teach mathematics as a biology major. At the time of writing this book, I serve as a district pastor working with two dedicated volunteer lay pastors, and a committed group leader to lead two churches and a group as I serve as a superintendent of schools. From time to time, I teach a course at Meadow View Junior Academy. So, I am a teacher and a pastor. Here I am calling pastors and schools the *big divide*.

In an article adapted from his keynote address to pastors and teachers at a conference pastor/teacher convention, Dr. George

---

[1] Shane Anderson, *How to Kill Adventist Education (and How to Give It a Fighting Chance)* (Hagerstown: Review and Herald Publishing Association, 2009), 25.

Knight expressed what he calls "an identity crisis for nearly my entire career."[1] To make the point clearer, Dr. Knight continues, "I suppose my psychological and professional problems would not be quite so acute if the two realms of my professional life had a little more contact with each other."[2] Very funny but true. This dilemma is what I call the big divide. This great Adventist historian takes it home as he always does when he states, "One of the most remarkable things about the Adventist subculture is that the only two professional groups that are employed in the local church full time in most congregations have little understanding, sympathy, or even contact with each other's ministries, trials, challenges, and contributions. That fact is more than remarkable; it is tragic![3]" Dr. Knight has a way of telling us the truth in a captivating manner that makes us think and laugh at the same time. I have enjoyed his classes at the seminary. He uses stories in history to connect us to the present as we learn from and about the past. This divide should not be, but sadly it exists. I believe the Seventh-day Adventist Church has created it and must correct it.

In that same article, after telling his audience how Martin Luther considered the work of the schoolteacher as "one of the highest virtues on earth," Dr. Knight turned to scriptures (Ephesians 4:11, RSV) where "Paul used a Greek construction that indicates that the office of pastor and teacher was held by the same person when he noted that 'some should be apostles, some prophets, some evangelists, some pastors and teachers.'"[4] He noted that these two gifts are not listed separately while the others are. He said, "Christian teachers function in a pastoral role to their students, and Christian pastors' function in a teaching role to their parishioners.[5]

I don't want to quote the entire keynote address, but I will only share the following:

> The major difference between the roles of pastors and teachers today has to do with the current division of labor. In 21st-century society, the Christian teacher is usually seen as someone who pastors in a "school" context, while the pastor is defined as someone who teaches in the "larger

religious community." However, their function is essentially the same, even though by today's definitions they are in charge of different divisions of the Lord's vineyard. That is why, with that biblical perspective in mind, I have chosen the title "Two Ministries/One Mission."[6]

Since I am writing as a Seventh-day Adventist pastor and teacher, I will continue to use the current divides between the pastoral and teaching ministries in the Seventh-day Adventist Church. At the same time, I am very mindful of other Christians from other denominations reading this book. I highly suggest that each denomination addresses this divide between pastors and teachers where it exists.

This proper scriptural understanding will help us bridge these two ministries in the way we work with each other and also in the way the Adventist Church treats pastors and teachers.

Let me be blunt. When I speak of pastors, I do not only speak of the local church pastors; I also speak of all pastors at different administrative roles in the Church. Most administrators were at one time pastors for the most part. I believe one of the reasons that church schools continue to struggle is because we do not have enough *champions* for church schools in the leadership of the Church, which is held by pastors, for the most part. We need pastors at every level of the Church administration who are champions for church schools, especially at the elementary and secondary levels.

Champions for Church Schools at the Elementary and Secondary Levels

We need pastors who are champions for church schools at the elementary and secondary levels. The *Merriam-Webster* defines the word *champions* in three different terms:[7] First, a champion is "a winner of first prize or first place in competition,"[8] although in the Adventist Church, a pastor receives a call to serve at a specific church. He or she receives the call after going through an interview process.

Similarly, church leaders or officers are called to serve after going through a nominating committee process. Those who have been selected or nominated are indeed champions or winners, although we expect them to model servant leadership. These individuals can be considered champions, as defined above.

Many local church pastors and other pastors who serve in various leadership levels in the Church have obtained these high positions in the Church promising to support Adventist education or our church schools but have not done any more than their predecessors. We have not seen any substantive change. It continues to be business as usual. The challenges in financing our schools persist even under new leadership. I have met very few pastors or church leaders who have questioned policies that have kept the appropriation or subsidies to our schools at a level that is not sustainable. These pastors are in the minority.

We have many champions who are winners of higher position in the Church but not champions for church schools. No church would hire a pastor if he or she at the interview shares his or her lack of enthusiasm for church schools. That is, assuming questions about church schools are part of the interview questions. Similarly, no constituent (state, regional, or even at the global level) would vote a president or an officer if he or she says upfront that church schools is not an essential ministry of the Church. These champions usually emerge under the umbrella of great evangelists, evangelists who will rebaptize our children after they have left the church but not evangelists who will question policies, change policies to give access to children in our schools, or keep them in church schools. These champions do not see church schools as evangelism, nor do they see our teachers as educational evangelists. It is not what one says but what one does. I hope to be proven wrong. Being wrong on this topic would mean more for our schools at every level. We need actions that will benefit our schools, actions that will give access to every church school age child in our church schools. We need more champions for our church schools.

Second, *Merriam-Webster* dictionary defines *champion* as "a militant advocate or defender." We need more militant advocates or defenders for our church schools. We need more pastors, state, regional, national, and global officers to be "militant advocates or defenders" for our church schools and for our children. Militant advocates or defenders usually go against the status quo. These are individuals who ask, "Why not?" Why not change these policies that we know are not working to provide enough funding to give access to more students to our schools? Why not change the financial subsidy to schools' formulas that have not been changed for years? Those militant advocates see our schools as eternal investments and not financial burdens on our Church. Militant advocates or defenders of church schools understand the challenges and help bring tangible solutions, sustainable solutions. They do not provide Band-Aids nor hide behind policies to give the minimal. Currently, we have too few champions in that category at each level. These individuals see the schools as an integral part of the Church. They do whatever it takes to keep the schools alive and well. I have met some but very few. I pray for more.

Third, *Merriam-Webster* dictionary defines *champion* as "WARRIOR, FIGHTER."[9] This type of champion is a difficult one to understand. When most of us think of warriors or fighters, we may think of anger or violence. These words do not seem too Christ-like. We are called to put on the full armor of God (Ephesians 6:10–18),[10] that is to be warriors. Paul uses the language or imagery of Roman soldiers asking us to be strong in the Lord. I do not want to preach. We need warriors and fighters for church schools. I have seen some but not too many. These individuals (church leaders and members alike) go beyond the call of duty to help our schools. They do not put their tenure or their reelection first when it comes to standing for our kids. They go beyond the policies.

These champions do what it takes to help our church schools. Budgets speak louder than words. You can see it in the local church budgets where they lead. You can see it in the budgets at the various levels of the Church where they serve. You can see it in their own home budgets. These warriors or fighters see our schools as their schools also. They see our students as their children. They don't see it as "this is the responsibility of the parents and not ours." They see these students as souls for Christ. Keeping them in our church schools may not put us on top of a best evangelists' or best pastors' list at any level of the Church organization, nor will it keep us on the union's best conference list. We need more warriors, fighters, and champions not in name but in action for church schools at the elementary and secondary levels.

Finally, *Merriam-Webster* dictionary defines a champion as "one that does battle for another's rights or honor."[11] Then added, "God will raise me up a *champion*—Sir Walter Scott,"[12] and I say, amen! We need every pastor to be such a champion for our schools. These champions cannot be hidden. May I and may you be one who fights for our schools, our kids, our teachers, and our principals. May we be the champions to see the children in need of a Christian education but not the irresponsibility of some parents. May we be the ones to speak for those with no voice yet. How I wish someone had spoken on my behalf when my family could not pay for my tuition at my church school as a child. May we be that one. Members, pastors, district conference leaders, union leaders, General Conference leaders need to do better. Let's do better because our schools deserve better. Our church schools *need* better.

Church leaders (and I am one) have created the big divide. I remember when I worked at Garden State Academy, I heard it said that if the academy is closed, the conference can hire more pastors. Pastors will have fewer churches. It became "us" versus "them." In researching for this chapter, I came across an article entitled, "The Same Gift: And to some...pastors and teachers."[13] In the article, Dr. Hoilette asks the question: "Is the pastoral ministry superior to the teaching ministry?" This question is one that I wish we did not have to even ask. I remember during my years as a principal, I visited the district churches quite often and became friends with many church leaders. Several of the members approached me suggesting that I should work as a pastor instead of a principal. One of them commented that the job of the pastor was more secured than that of the principal. I knew he was right. This is the unfortunate reality that we, church leaders, have created in the church. Teachers are concerned about their yearly employment, which is linked to the school enrollment. Pastors seem not to have such a concern about their reemploy-ment. We need to do better for our teachers if we value their ministry as ministers, as educational evangelists. We need to do better for our schools.

Dr. Hoilette writes: "A number of educators have felt that the church treated pastoral ministry as superior to teaching ministry. However, this does seem to be changing. The teaching ministry has received some recognition (albeit sometimes grudgingly and patron-izingly). Actions and pronouncements by church administrators, who are mainly ordained ministers, have acknowledged the impor-tance of Christian teachers in fulfilling the gospel commission. The 'Commissioned Teacher' designation is one example of an attempt to align teaching with ministry." The article was published in December 1992/January 1993. This indicated period is a long time ago in the timeline of many. The article presents a well-balanced assessment, so I do not want to misrepresent this great work. However, many years later, we are still not there. We need to find ways to correct this. Our actions speak louder than words. Many who are reading this book can do something about it. Let's be champions for Christian educa-tion or church schools!

I came across another excellent article on the subject of pastors and schools entitled: "Pastors and Schools—The Dream Team."[14] The author, Kerosoma, another brilliant mind, states at the begin-ning of the article that "pastors can and do serve in many roles at Seventh-day Adventist schools. Board chair, speaker at week of prayer, counselor, transportation coordinator for service projects, softball pitcher at recess, Bible teacher, fundraiser for the worthy stu-dent fund, and director of Bible studies for baptismal class are only a partial list of ways that pastors contribute to their local Adventist school."[15] I praise God for the many pastors who have filled those roles and much more. We need more. The success of the local church school can be attributed to the involvement of the pastors in their schools. Please note that I say, "pastors." Most of our schools have more than a pastor in their school district or constituency. My wife, like many other principals, can use more pastoral help. I am very thankful and praise God for the involvement of many pastors in our schools. I must say that we have too many pastors who are not yet involved.

As a superintendent of schools, I attend many board meetings. There are pastors who are not only in attendance regularly at school board meetings but are also involved in the schools. On the other hand, I have to apologize to board members for the lack of pastors' attendance and involvement at schools. If we expect the church members to show interest in our schools, pastors must set examples. Our teachers and principals need the support of our pastors. Show me a school that is supported by its pastors, and I will show you a successful school financially and enrollment wise. When the school is supported by the pastors, the church members also support the school.

Kerosoma (December 2008/January 2009) also provides a list of how the school can get pastors involved:[16]

- Ask the pastor to establish prayer teams in his or her church(es) that have a designated time each day when they pray for the school and staff.
- Suggest that the pastor deploy local elders to dialogue with the school on how church can provide support, even if resources are limited. This could include work bees, assisting in the classroom, or recruiting students.
- Invite the pastor to join the students for lunch on a certain day each week or to help supervise sports or field trips.
- Ask the pastor to find creative ways to involve students in church leadership, worship services, and overall church life.
- Offer the teachers and principal as possible worship and prayer meeting speakers at the local church(es).
- Work with the pastor to arrange for the students' artwork to be posted in the church atrium, and for school events to be featured in the bulletin.
- Regularly send notes from students and staff affirming the local pastors' ministry and telling them that you are praying for them.

I must share this positive story. When I first became principal, I met this great pastor that I aspire to emulate. He came to me and said something like (I paraphrase), "Sadrail, you have my support. If anybody from my church wants to send their children to this school, know that their tuition will be paid for." Well, guess what? He kept his words. I sent many families to his church. All their children's tuitions were paid for in full. How much we have missed him when he left our conference. Christian education or church schools need more of such pastors!

I have seen more of a picture of the big divide instead of a dream team. Let's do something to change this for our children and our schools. Thank you to all the pastors who have supported our schools. We are in the same team. Better yet, the same family. I will end this chapter with a list from the North American Division School Board Manual 2018 regarding the pastor's relationship to the school:[17] It states: "The pastor(s) serves a vital role in strengthening Adventist education." The pastor's involvement often includes:

- Leadership and support of Adventist education by precept and example.
- Church involvement in the financial support of the school.
- Encouragement of effective parent, teacher, and pupil relationships.
- Assisting in the spiritual emphasis of the school.
- Involvement as a spiritual counselor and resource person.
- Promoting recognition of administrator(s) and faculty as educational leaders.
- Fulfilling an advisory role to the school board and staff. Serving as an *ex officio* member of the school board with voting privileges. It is recommended that the pastor not serve as chair of the school board.

The manual continues: "When the relationship between the board chair and pastor is strong, both school and church benefit. When the relationship is challenged, more often than not, both school and church suffer." It also provides important "tips" that can foster a healthy board chair-pastor relationship:

- Communication should be substantive, timely, and transparent.
- Meetings, whether board and/or finance committee, that address school budget, school capital projects, and other financial matters that could impact the church budget should always involve the pastor (or designee).
- Privileged information regarding school and/or church families/members should never be compromised by either party except in cases that involve a child's safety or well-being is at stake or must give way to the requirements of the law, e.g., suspected child abuse.
- School and church board meetings should never involve "surprise" agenda items for either the board chair (at church board meetings) or pastor (at school board meetings).
- The pastor should not chair either the school board or its finance committee.
- Significant differences of opinion on school related matters that cannot be resolved between the board chair (or board as a whole) and the pastor(s) should be taken to the superintendent of education and, if necessary, to the conference board of education to facilitate resolution.
- Under no circumstances should one, publicly or privately, diminish the other regardless of the issues at hand.

CHAPTER 8

CHURCHES AND SCHOOLS: THEIR PURPOSE AND GOALS

What Every Church and School Need to Know

And Jesus came and spake unto them, saying,
All power is given unto me in heaven and in
earth. Go ye therefore, and teach all nations,
baptizing them in the name of the Father, and
of the Son, and of the Holy Ghost; teaching
them to observe all things whatsoever I have
commanded you; and, lo, I am with you always,
even unto the end of the world. Amen.
—Matthew 28:18–20 (KJV)

The Adult Sabbath School Bible Study Guide for Seventh-day Adventists for the last quarter of 2020 was dedicated to Education. The selection of this topic has highlighted once again the Church's commitment to Christian education. The study guide utilized material from the book *Education* (1903) by Ellen G. White. *Education* was dedicated as follows: "To parents, teachers, and students, all pupils in earth's preparatory school, this book is dedicated. May it aid them in securing life's greatest benefits, development, and joy in service here, and thus a fitness for that wider service, the "higher course" open to every human being in the school of the hereafter."[1] The book, in a sense, was dedicated to everyone for we are all "pupils in earth's preparatory school." In order words, it was dedicated to every church member.

Since the Adult Sabbath School Study Guide serves as a tool to instruct the Seventh-day Adventist world church through a systematic study of the Bible,[2] it was long overdue for the Church to study the topic of Christian or Church school education. At the end of the introduction of the Study Guide, the following two questions were posed: "What does it mean to have a 'Christian education,' and how can we as a church, in one way or another, find a way so that all our members are able to get such an education?" (p. 3).

A few years ago, I attended a church board meeting, and one of the board members asked me, "Why Seventh-day Adventist schools since we have so many other schools?" The board member's question gave me the opportunity to explain the reason for church schools. We have a lot of work to do to educate the church members in our pews about the purpose for our church schools.

In 2017, Dr. Beardsley-Hardy, the director of the Department of Education of the General Conference of Seventh-day Adventists, wrote a report on the state of Seventh-day Adventist education.[3] In that report, she outlined data reported in the Annual Statistical Reports of the Seventh-day Adventist Church in 2015, which revealed "that less than half of church membership had some Adventist education (47 percent), and 52 percent had none. More than half of the membership have not attended a Seventh-day Adventist school."[4] While the main focus of the article was to shed light on the enrollment challenges in Adventist education worldwide, the point can also be made to the difficulties of educating our Church members on the purpose of Adventist education in order to support its mission which is the same as the mission of the Church emphasizing that "the work of redemption and education are one, and that the Seventh-day Adventist Church is a movement of prophecy with an end time mission to all the world."[5]

The article entitled "Education for What? Thoughts on the Purpose and Identity of Adventist Education"[6] by one of the Adventist

Church historians, George Knight, would have been very appropriate for the church member that I mentioned earlier. I have learned not to assume that the Adventist Church members and local church leaders know *why* Adventist education. This incident took place before the publication of the fourth quarter of the Adult Sabbath School Bible Study entitled "Education."[7] I am glad now that every church member is aware of the purpose of our schools. Or do they?

Like many educators, I was delighted to see the Sabbath School quarterly on *Education*. I approached the quarterly with high expectations that our church members would be educated on the value of church schools and how to support it. It was noted from the onset that the Adult Sabbath School Bible Study Guide had been written by various presidents of Seventh-day Adventist colleges and universities in North America (p. 3). Their names were not listed. I am grateful for their work.

After studying and analyzing this Adult Sabbath School Bible Study Guide (2020), I believe it is fair to say that our church members and leaders, assuming that they studied the lessons, are very aware of what Christian education should be. It was noted that "because the Lord is the source of all true knowledge, all true education, all Christian education should direct our minds toward Him and toward His own revelation about Himself" (p. 3). I would add that this is what our church schools have been doing through the years in the North American Division and throughout the world Church.

The vision and mission of Adventist education are expressed as follows: "To enable learners to develop a life of faith in God, and to use their knowledge, skills, and understandings to serve God and humanity"[8] and "for every learner to excel in faith, learning, and service, blending biblical truth and academic achievement to honor God and bless others."[9] It is my prayer that this section of the book serves as a supplement to the Sabbath School Bible Study Guide on Education by connecting Christian Education and our church schools for our members. Again, I am very grateful for the lesson study on *Education* because now we know that every member of the Seventh-day Adventist Church has been instructed on Christian education as defined by Ellen G. White.

After graduating from the seminary at Andrews University, I received the call to serve as a Bible teacher and chaplain. I needed to take several education courses to obtain my teaching certificate. In one of the education courses, I learned a teaching strategy called K-W-L (Know, Want to Know, Learned).[10] It is described as follows: "K-W-L (Ogle 1986) is an instructional reading strategy that is used to guide students through a text. Students begin by brainstorming everything they Know about a topic. This information is recorded in the K column of a K-W-L chart. Students then generate a list of questions about what they Want to Know about the topic. These questions are listed in the W column of the chart. During or after reading, students answer the questions that are in the W column. This new information that they have Learned is recorded in the L column of the K-W-L chart."[11]

Using K-W-L as a Guide

In the next section, I will list the materials from the Sabbath School Bible Study Guide on Education to recap what our church members Know (K) about Christian Education. This method will be true also for those who have also read the book *Education* by Ellen G. White since the Study Guide was based on that same book. Then, I will introduce a section of what I want my readers to know, which can serve as a refresher for those who have read the book *Education* or study the Study Guide, and I am sure there are many who know more of the topic than I do. Then, I will present a short summary of what I think we have gone over. In actual K-W-L, it would be students sharing what they *K*now; *W*ant to know; and what they have *L*earned. I used this strategy to help me organize the materials that I am presenting. I ask for forgiveness to those who are skilled in using K-W-L.

What every Seventh-day Adventist Church member should Know
(for K in K-W-L) about "True Education" from studying the
fourth quarter 2020 Adult Sabbath School Study Guide

- True Education—"Scripture is clear: 'God is love' (1 John 4:8), which explains this quote from Ellen G. White, "Love, the basis of creation and of redemption, is the basis of true education." (*Education,* 16)
- Because the Lord is the source of all true knowledge, all true education, all Christian education should direct our minds toward Him and toward His own revelation about Himself. (p. 3)
- Even nature, so defiled by thousands of years of sin, still speaks, even powerfully, of the goodness and character of God when studied from the perspective given us in Scripture. But the Written Word, the Scriptures, is the perfect standard of truth, the greatest revelation we have of who God is and what He has done and is doing for humanity. Scripture, and its message of Creation and Redemption, must be central to all Christian education. (p. 3)
- Thus, whatever else Christian education entails, it must obviously seek to help students better understand the light that God offers us from heaven. (p. 3)
- The good news is that because of Jesus and the plan of redemption, all is not lost. We have hope of salvation and of restoration. And much of Christian education should be pointing students toward Jesus and what He has done for us and the restoration that He offers. (p. 10)
- True education will lead to true knowledge, the knowledge of Christ, and thus not only will we become more like Him, but we also

may stand to share our knowledge of Him with others. (p. 10)

- And, since the despising of authority is so condemned, shouldn't our Christian education also consist of learning the right way to understand, submit, and obey "those who rule over you" (Heb. 13:7, NKJV)? (p. 11)
- Christian education is a commitment to educating families and members in doctrine, worship, instruction, fellowship, evangelism, and service. (p. 15)
- No; the law also is there to point us to the way of life, which is found only in Jesus. This also is what true education should be about, pointing us to a life of grace, of faith, and of obedience to Christ. (p. 22)
- Just as ancient Israel would prosper by obeying God's law (even though they needed grace, as well), it's no different for us today either. Hence, as part of Christian education we need to keep God's law as a central component of what it means to live by faith and trusting in God's grace. (p. 25)
- "Love, the basis of creation and of redemption, is the basis of true education. This is made plain in the law that God has given as the guide of life. The first and great commandment is, "Thou shalt love the Lord thy God with all thy heart, and with all thy soul, and with all thy strength, and with all thy mind" (Luke 10:27). To love Him, the infinite, the omniscient One, with the whole strength, and mind, and heart, means the highest development of every power. It means that in the whole being—

the body, the mind, as well as the soul—the image of God is to be restored (p. 28).

- Central to any Christian education is the reality, not just of God but of the kind of God that He is, a personal God who loves us and who interacts with us. He is a God of miracles who, though using natural laws, is not bound by those laws and who can transcend those laws when He wills (such as in the virgin conception of Jesus). The teaching of this view is especially pertinent in our day because so much of the intellectual world, claiming (erroneously) that science supports it, openly and unapologetically teaches the atheistic and naturalistic worldview. (p. 31)

- The doctrine of Creation also is foundational to any Christian education. Everything we believe as Christians, everything, rests on the doctrine of the six-day Creation. The Bible didn't begin with a statement about atonement, or about the law, or about the Cross, or about the Resurrection, or about the Second Coming. (p. 32)

- As Seventh-day Adventists, we must firmly adhere to the teachings of the Bible, for this is God's revealed truth to humans, explaining for us many things about the world that we would otherwise not know or understand. Hence, all Christian education must be rooted and grounded in the Word of God, and any teaching contrary to it must be rejected. (p. 33)

- Before He has spoken His first parable or performed His first miracle, the Master Teacher is worthy of our worship because of who He is. To fully appreciate the later teaching ministry of Jesus, we must join these early pupils, the wise men, in their worship of the Master Teacher. The one whose teachings we admire is more than a wise educator. He is God come to dwell with humankind. Christian education is rooted in the worship of Christ. (p. 43)

- "In the Teacher sent from God, all true educational work finds its center. Of this work today as verily as of the work He established eighteen hundred years ago, the Saviour speaks in the words—"I am the First and the Last, and the Living One." (p. 44)

- Of course, that's one reason the gospel is universal, and Christ's death was for all humanity. Whatever our differences, surely one thing unites us: our general sinfulness. Hence, true Christian education must be about pointing us to the only solution for our rather dismal state. This week we'll look at our only solution, our Master Teacher. (p. 46)

- Whatever else Christian education entails, why must it entail, even emphasize, the fact that our natural state is to hide from God, and then point us to Jesus as the solution? (p. 47)

- Hence, because worship is so central to the Christian experience, Christian education must deal with the question of worship, the subject for this week's lesson. (p. 56)

- The three Jewish boys obviously took the second commandment (Exod. 20:4–6) as seriously as God had meant it to be taken. After all, it's part of the Ten

Commandments, right up there with prohibitions on murder and robbery and so forth. Worship, proper worship, is so important that, in fact, it becomes central to the issues in the last days, before the second coming of Christ. Thus, Christian education needs to include the whole question of worship: what is it, how do we do it, why is it important, and whom do we worship? (p. 57)

- Many of the great intellectual ideas in the world today are based on a naturalistic view of reality. Many disciplines studied in school today are studied from that perspective, which often means that what is taught will be contradictory to Scripture. We can be tempted to worship ideas that have been postulated, theorized, and put into practice. We also can deify the brilliant minds of the philosophers, scientists, and mathematicians who trademarked these ideas. The problem is that often these ideas can clash with Scripture, yet because they are now currently taught and believed to be true, people try to incorporate them into Christian education. However, the only way that can be done is to compromise the faith, which often means twisting and distorting the Scriptures in order to try to make Scripture fit with current ideas. (p. 61)

- The Bible story is not unlike our own human stories that we know so well—with one exception. The story of God and His people is assured of a good ending, of reaching its goal. Divine grace toward His people assures that outcome. The human responsibility in this relationship has often been misunderstood and even dreaded by many who have thought of it as onerous. But in fact, the Bible story is essentially an invitation to know God and understand His will. Indeed, learning to know God is our foremost response to His grace. We cannot earn such grace, but we can learn about it, and what is Christian education if not, at its core, education teaching us about this grace? (p. 64)

- The story of Redemption is a story of education from Creation to Incarnation, and from Incarnation to re-creation. God is a teacher, and heaven is a school for all time (see Ellen G. White, Education, p. 301). What are the implications of this thought for our commitment to Christian education at home, in church, in school, in the university, and throughout life? (p. 65)

- True Christian education, if nothing else, must cause us to rise above these human foibles and evils, and see others as Christ sees them, beings for whom He died, beings whose sins He bore on the cross, beings for whom He paid an infinite price. If we uplift the cross, as we must, then we will see the value and worth of every human being and, ideally, treat them as they truly deserve, in keeping with the value that God has placed on them. Christian education must include this teaching or else it is not worthy of the name "Christian." (p. 73)

- And yet, here was Jesus, calling them to live as light. To be merciful. To be pure in heart. To be makers of peace. Christian education must, then, include teaching our students to be lights in the world, to be able to make choices and decisions that will reveal the reality and goodness of God to others (p. 74).

- If the church is serious about being a force for Christian education, it is imperative that we begin with Jesus. Jesus called disciples. He trained them to do mission by walking with them. Jesus provided opportunity for them to be involved in the lives of people whom they were to care for and to love. And daily Jesus challenged them by His vision of what this world could be when people begin to treat each other as brothers and sisters. (p. 75)

- Hence, all Christian education must include this sense of mission, of purpose, not just to earn a living but to do in our own sphere what Jesus calls us to do: to follow in His footsteps of ministering to those in need, and to share with them the good news of the gospel. (p. 75)

- And, of course, here is where Scripture plays the central role. Who are we? Why are we here? How should we live? What happens when we die? Why is there evil and suffering? These are the questions that seekers of truth have been asking since the beginning of recorded history. What a privilege, and what a responsibility, to be able to help point these seekers toward some answers now. What is Christian education if not pointing people to these answers, as found in the Word of God? (p. 75)

- Education includes what has been called "the arts and sciences." But when we learn or teach the arts and sciences from a biblical perspective, what does this imply? Are we simply offering select Bible verses that relate to a particular aspect of modern medicine or art history, for example? In so doing, we can relate our practical lessons to the amazing power of God in creating our complex world. But a simple incorporation of Scripture in a textbook lesson is only a small part of true education—the education that is salvific and redemptive. (p. 80)

- Especially in a day and age in which many humans have come to worship the creation rather than the Creator, how crucial that Christian education in the arts and sciences always work from the assumption that God is the Creator and Sustainer of all that exists. In the end, any ideologies and presuppositions that deny or exclude God can lead only to error. Worldly education all but works on the assumption of no God; Christian education must not fall into that trap, nor must it work even more subtly from the principles based on the assumption that there is no God. Either way, humans are bound to wind up in error. (p. 81)

- As with everything God has done, we have an enemy who distorts and exploits it. It shouldn't be surprising, then, that beauty and concepts of beauty can be used against us, as well. Thus, especially in the arts, Christian education, guided by Scripture, must help us learn to be careful in understanding that not all that is beautiful is necessarily good or holy. (p. 82)

- Biological science today, for instance, is predicated on the assumption that life began billions of years ago, by chance, with no God and no purpose behind it. At the same time, an incredible amount of complicated and detailed scientific literature has arisen based on this teaching. What lessons can we take away from this about how people can be experts in error? How should this realization impact Christian education in general and the teaching of science in particular? (p. 83)

- The problem, however, is that Scripture teaches that God not only created everything but that He sustains everything, as well. This means that any true Christian education in science would have to work from radically different assumptions than what science in general claims. Inevitably, clashes will occur, especially when it comes to origins. (p. 85)

- Work—a curse or a blessing? It seemed to come as part of the curse of sin (Gen. 3:17). A closer reading reveals it was the ground that was cursed, and not the work. Ellen G. White states that God intended this commission to work as a blessing: "The life of toil and care which was henceforth to be man's lot was appointed in love. It was a discipline rendered needful by his sin, to place a check upon the indulgence of appetite and passion, to develop habits of self-control. It was a part of God's great plan for man's recovery from the ruin and degradation of sin" (*Patriarchs and Prophets*, p. 60). Might we perhaps have made it a curse through monotony, overwork, or overvaluing its role in our lives? Whatever our situation, we must learn to put work in its proper perspective. And Christian education must help train people to learn the value of work, while at the same time not making an idol out of it (p. 94).

Reflection and Follow-up: What I believe every church member Wants to know (using K-W-L)

I believe the Adult Sabbath School Bible Study Guide for the last quarter of 2020 on *Education* instructed Seventh-day Adventist Church members on the meaning of Christian education, one of the questions that it intended to answer when it asked in the introduction "what does it mean to have a 'Christian education.'" The second part of the question which was "and how can we as a church, in one way or another, find a way so that all our members are able to get such an education?" (p. 3) had also been answered but not in the context of providing church schools for our precious children and youth. In the rest of this chapter, I endeavor to offer some practical suggestions based on *Testimonies to the Church, Volume 6* on the chapter entitled "Church Schools" (pp. 193–218), where Ellen G. White provided such instructions. I will also add a few comments as an educator and pastor.

The Work of the Church Schools

The chapter begins as follows: "The church has a special work to do in educating and training its children that they may not, in attending school, or in any other association, be influenced by those of corrupt habits" (p. 193). This is a very powerful and important statement. Note that Ellen White (1903) writes "the church," which is composed of all of us, not just the parents. It is the "special work" of the church to educate and train its children in the ways of the Lord

(Proverbs 22:6, Isaiah 54:13). Even in her days, Ellen White wrote: "The world is full of iniquity and disregard of the requirements of God" (p. 193). The world has *certainly* not gotten better. We must all agree that the world has gotten *worse*. She asked the following questions: "Do our children receive from the teachers in the public schools [sic] ideas that are in harmony with the word of God? Is sin presented as an offense against God? Is obedience to all the commandments of God taught as the beginning of all wisdom?" (p. 193). The answers are still and will remain no for every public school and non-Christian school regardless of their locations or zip codes in the United States and in many parts of the world.

In the article entitled "What Makes Christian Education Distinct,"[12] Hendricks states that Christian education takes a higher perspective. He writes, "In Christian education we deal with the transcendent. Secular education deals only with the human. Christian education discusses the eternal, secular education the here and now."[13] Anderson, in the book *How to Kill Adventist Education (and How to Give It a Fighting Chance!)* defines *secularism* "as the mode of thought that sees God as either removed from or optional to daily living. The individual (as the final arbiter of what constitutes "truth"), not God, determines how he or she should live. Morality predictably declines in such mindset, as the human proclivity to do evils set free to choose one's path"[14] (p. 51). In that vein, public education in the United States is secular in nature for religion or God is not taught there. Religion, which is defined as the service and worship of God or the supernatural or commitment or devotion to religious faith or observance,[15] is not taught in public schools. Faith in God is not taught in public schools. Knight writes, "One of the more problematic aspects of public education is the place of the "fourth R"—religion"[16] (p. 267). God and religion are not the focus of secular education. Conversely, Knight writes, "Since the function of Christian education is one of reconciliation and restoring the balanced image of God in students, education should be seen primarily as a redemptive act"[17] (pp. 210, 211). The Christian Church must make it its duty to ensure that the children of the Church receive the "true education," as stated by Ellen White. Such "true education" is found only in church schools where children are taught by God.

Ellen G. White continues, "We send our children to the Sabbath school that they may be instructed in regard to the truth, and then as they go to the day school, lessons containing falsehood are given them to learn. These things confuse the mind, and should not be; for if the young receive ideas that pervert the truth, how will the influence of this education be counteracted?" (pp. 193, 194). The Seventh-day Adventist Church, like many of other Christian denominations, establish church schools so that our children can be taught of the Lord 24/7 (in the home, church, and school). Children and youth in Adventist schools are educated by Seventh-day Adventist teachers with Seventh-day Adventist curricula. I dare say that Adventist schools or Christian schools in general should not exist for only those who can afford to pay the tuition. It should be accessible to all in the same way that the Sabbath School or Sunday school is accessible to all.

As I stated earlier in the book, when I preach at a Seventh-day Adventist Church on the topic of church schools on a given Sabbath, I usually ask the church members to tell me the time. Then, I ask them what day it is today? Then, I say, "It is Sabbath and (time), do you know where your children's teachers and principals are?" I usually recount the story as told by one of my favorite professors and writers, Dr. George Knight, in the article entitled "Why Have Adventist Education."[18] He wrote: "Don't let anyone tell you that the school one attends makes no difference. The power of education was forcefully brought to my attention as a young pastor in Galveston, Texas. One of my professional families wanted to keep their only daughter near to them, so they sent her to the very fine local Roman Catholic school. It is perhaps not altogether surprising, given the power of education, that she dedicated her adult life to being a nun."[19] This illustrates the power of education.

My wife, as I stated earlier in the book, serves as a principal/teacher at a Seventh-day Adventist school. One of the families at her school was very concerned about sending their child to another Christian school in their community to complete grades 11 and 12 since the school where my wife works only offers an online option to students in grades 11 and 12. The family was concerned with the doctrinal belief differences between the Seventh-day Adventist Church and the other Christian denomination where their child would be attending. The family reluctantly sends their child to another Christian school. At that school, the family sees a banner with the following message: "You send our children to be educated by Caesar then act surprised when they come out talking like a Roman." Baucham (2007), in the book *Family Driven Faith—Doing What It Takes to Raise Sons and Daughters who Walk with God,* illustrates this very clear when he writes:

> Christian education is a critical tool in the culture war. More importantly, it is a critical tool in the evangelism and discipleship of the next generation. This is evidenced by Jesus' words in Luke 6:40, "A pupil is not above his teacher; but everyone, after he has been fully trained, will be like his teacher." Even Muslims understand the power of Christian education. Sheikh Ahmad Al Katani, in an interview on the infamous Al Jazeera television network, responded to the fact that six million African Muslims a year are converting to Christianity. According to Katani, the culprit is not large evangelistic crusades but Christian education." (p. 209)

Thus, Christian education is evangelism and contributes to making disciples of our children and youth. Baucham continues, "contrary to popular opinion, there is no such thing as amoral education. All education reaches one's view of God, man, truth, knowledge, and ethics from the educational process. Every day that our children sit behind a desk, they are either being taught to know, love, and obey God or they are being taught to love and obey someone or something that has usurped God's proper role" (p. 127).

Let me introduce here an article by another brilliant mind of our Church, Dr. John Wesley Taylor V. The article is entitled,

"Joining and Remaining: A Look at the Data on the Role of Adventist Education."[20] In this article, Dr. Taylor not only responded to the questions by many parents on whether Adventist education makes a difference but also by pastors and other church leaders: "Is Adventist education truly evangelism? Does it justify the resources that we invest? If so, how can we present a persuasive case for Adventist education to parents and other church members?"

- Is it effective? Each year for the past 10 years, there have been at least 30,000 and in some years, more than 50,000 students in Adventist schools baptized during the school year, primarily in culminating events such as a Week of Prayer. The total for the 2006–2015 period was 427,313 baptisms[6]. To look at it another way, this is equivalent to a typical-size conference being established each year through the evangelistic ministry of Adventist education.

- A 1990 study, for example, analyzed 844 children and youth from Adventist families in the Southern Union Conference of the North American Division.[7] Of those children and youth who had no Adventist education, 40.1 percent were never baptized. Of those with one or more years of Adventist education, 15.4 percent were never baptized; while in the group with 11 or more years of Adventist education, only 3.1 percent were never baptized.

- Another study conducted in 1985 of 807 children and youth from Adventist families in the Lake Union Conference of the North American Division found similar results.[8] Of those children and youth with no Adventist education, 38.3 percent never joined the church. In the group with some Adventist education, 4.6 percent never joined the church, while 100 percent of those in the sample who studied all 12 grades in Adventist education joined the church.

- One of the largest studies was the set of Valuegenesis surveys, conducted over a 20-year period, from 1990 to 2010.[13] Valuegenesis[1] data from 2,267 12th-grade Adventist students in Adventist schools in the North American Division, for example, showed that the more years of Adventist schooling, the greater the person's reported loyalty to the Seventh-day Adventist Church, his or her belief in the fundamental teachings of the church, and his or her intention to remain an Adventist at age 40. In the 2010 Valuegenesis[3] survey, 81 percent of all students indicated that attending an Adventist school was the most important factor that had helped them develop their religious faith, with the Adventist school ranking more highly than any other factor (see Figure 3). Across all three Valuegenesis studies (1990–2010), a full 75 percent of Adventist students in Adventist schools believed that the chances of their remaining in the Adventist Church at age 40 were good to excellent.

- We have noted the Youth Retention study, which endeavored to follow high school students for 10 years, utilizing a sample about evenly divided between students in Adventist schools and in non-Adventist schools in the U.S. and Canada. One of the key findings of this research was that the number of years in an Adventist school was positively related to commitment to Jesus Christ and to commitment to personal Bible study, as well as to the statements "My relationship with Christ is stronger now" and "Religion is important in my life."[14] Furthermore, intention to marry an Adventist in students who attended an Adventist school was nearly twice the proportion of those who had not attended an Adventist school (83 percent vs. 46 percent, respectively). At the 10-year mark, the probability of leaving the Adventist Church was 3.9 times greater for those who had attended non-Adventist schools, compared to those who had attended Seventh-day Adventist schools.

Dr. Taylor concluded: "Adventist education is a consistent and important predictor of children and youth joining and remaining in the Seventh-day Adventist Church. As Ellen White observed: 'In the highest sense, the work of education and the work of redemption are one.'[22] In essence, Adventist education is mission. Through Adventist education, children and youth experience accession and retention for the ultimate purpose of redemption. Consequently, the Seventh-day Adventist Church must reaffirm and uplift the central role of Adventist education in the evangelistic mission of the Church."[21]

In the same chapter of "Church Schools," in *Testimonies for the Church, Volume 6*, Ellen G. White, in dealing with "The Children Neglected,"[22] writes: "All the youth should be permitted to have the blessings and privileges of an education at our schools, that they may be inspired to become laborers together with God" (p. 197). Then, she addressed the necessity for our church schools. Ellen G. White went as far as recommending that "in localities where there is a church, schools should be established if there are no more than six children to attend" (p. 199). She continues, "Work as if you were working for your life to save the children from being drowned in the polluting, corrupting, influences of the world" (p. 199). Ellen White was writing to the Adventist Church members. She was addressing church members and leaders alike.

The Seventh-day Adventist Church, like other Christian churches, must then make it a priority to establish schools in very locality to ensure that our children receive a Christian education, the "true education," as per Ellen White. She saw it as being the "duty" of the church when she wrote: "We are far behind our duty in this important matter" (p. 199). Every Seventh-day Adventist child and youth deserve an Adventist education. Every Christian child deserves a Christian education. It is the duty of the church to make it a priority to ensure it happens. She called on the church to repent: "But though in the past we have come short of doing what we might have done for the youth and children, let us now repent and redeem the time" (p. 200). "The churches are to assist worthy students as it is a solemn responsibility for the churches to train the children and youth" (p. 213). "The churches should feel it a privilege to take a part in defraying the expenses" (p. 213) of the students who are unable to pay.

For elementary and secondary Christian schools to be successful, they need the financial support of every church and church member. Ellen White writes: "Let all share the expense" (p. 217). As church members, "we cannot call ourselves true missionaries if we neglect those at our very doors who are at the most critical age and who need our aid to secure knowledge and experience that will fit them for the service of God" (p. 217).

In summary, which I will use as what we have Learned in K-W-L, our church schools are necessary. Our children and youth should attend our church schools. It is the duty of the church to provide church schools for the children and youth in our churches, regardless of their families' financial status. As indicated by Dr. Taylor, cited earlier in this chapter, "Writing to church leaders and educators, Ellen White declared that the all-important issue in Adventist education is the conversion of the student."[1] Based on the data shared in this chapter, "Through Adventist education, children and youth experience accession and retention, for the ultimate purpose of redemption."[23] Our Christian schools serve as effective tools for the evangelizing and discipling of our children and youth. The churches and church members are to help make our schools financially successful so that every child can attend our church schools. A special thank you to every church and church member for their support to our church schools. We also invite those who have not yet supported to join us in this endeavor. Become a champion for our church schools.

CHAPTER 9

SCHOOL BOARDS: PERCEPTION OF TRUTH IS EVERYTHING

But the one who does not know and does
things deserving punishment will be beaten
with few blows. From everyone who has
been given much, much will be demanded;
and from the one who has been entrusted
with much, much more will be asked.
—Luke 12:48 (NIV)

Early in my career as a superintendent of schools, I was blessed to attend a school leadership conference by Independent School Management (ISM). During the conference, one of the presenters in addressing school boards stated that board members are responsible for the continuity of the school. Their job is to make sure that the school exists for the children of the students who are currently attending the school. I was blown away by this thought. Perhaps I had heard it before but had missed it entirely. I have worked with many boards before. A lot of board members play a very passive role. Sometimes, jokingly, they are referred to as "report-receiving board members." Some are very involved. Sometimes their involvement is more to control the principal and the teachers. Other board members have been genuinely supportive of principals, teachers, and the mission and vision of the schools where they serve. These board members are champions for the schools. They recruit students for the school, serve as advocates for the schools at their churches, conferences, and communities. They contribute financially to the school on a regular basis. They consistently raise funds for the schools. They make friends for the school. They find volunteers for the school and volunteer in areas where they can at the school. I have met a few of these board members. I praise the Lord for them. We need more of them. Every board member should be a champion for his or her school.

I am aware of excellent board training resources produced by the Seventh-day Adventist Church. I will name a few. *Governing Boards: A Practical Guides to Best Practices and Policies*[1] produced in 2008 by the Columbia Union Education Department under the leadership of Dr. Hamlet Canosa. Most, if not all, unions have produced their own board manuals, which include their education codes to "assist individuals to become effective school board members and provide boards with the tools to operate successfully."[2] The *Manual for School Boards of Seventh-day Adventist Schools*[3] was produced by the North American Division in 2018. Most recently, during the first quarter of 2019, *The Journal of Adventist Education* published a special issue on School Boards,[4] which was coordinated by Dr. Bordes Henry Saturné.

After reading these excellent resources, I felt inadequate to address the topic because of the excellent materials that the Adventist Church already has on the subject by these brilliant minds. However, in this section, I will focus more on board members as champions for their Christian schools or church schools, Adventist schools in my context, to ensure the continuity of our elementary and secondary church schools as well as giving access to our schools to the children of the members of our churches who are not able to attend due to finances.

Selection and Duty of Adventist School Board Members

I am not sure how board members are selected in other Christian schools. According to the *Seventh-day Adventist Church Manual*, school board members are elected by the church or churches for elementary schools and junior academies.[5] It also states that the "division working policies explain the functions of school boards. School board members should be chosen for their consecration, their belief in and loyalty to the principles of Christian education, their good judgment and tact, their experience in school matters, and their financial judgment and ability. They should believe in and be willing to follow denominational educational policies and recommendations."[6] Board members in Adventist elementary and secondary schools do not run for the position like most public-school board members in the United States.[7] Serving on a board of an Adventist school is a call to serve the church in ministry. The school board is an essential component in maintaining a quality school program.[8] As part of the various ministries of the Church, the *Seventh-day Adventist Church Manual* also states that "the church elects an education secretary to promote and generate support for Christian education,"[9] which is also the role for every board member. It was noted that "in 2016, both chief executives and board chairs ranked fundraising as one of the weakest areas of board performance, along with other external responsibilities such as advocacy and community building and outreach."[10] These are vital areas that can assure the sustainability of our church schools in terms of recruiting and funding.

I dream of a time when Christian school boards, Adventist school boards in my context, will be involved in fundraising in order to keep every student in our schools instead of developing policies to remove students from our schools because their families cannot pay the tuition. Sometimes I wonder if the church school is a ministry of the Church since only those who can afford it, for the most part can partake of it. Imagine coming to Sabbath School on a Sabbath morning or to the Sunday School on a Sunday to be told that you cannot attend because you have not paid your church dues. This idea would be absurd while this is what many Christian school boards have voted to do. I know that schools have bills to pay. I also know that there are parents who are irresponsible with their finances. However, when a child is removed from a church school because the family did not or could not meet its financial obligations, the child is hurt, although he or she had no say in the matter. Furthermore, we have removed the child from the opportunity of being taught in the way of the Lord, which is also our duty as a Church, as stated earlier.

I know this is a complex and controversial topic. Perhaps having read my story about being sent home from a Seventh-day Adventist school as a child, one may say that I am still not over it, which is not so. On the contrary, I would like to use my experience to appeal to board members and church leaders to ensure that our children are given access to join and or remain in our church schools through the work of boards, making it their business to work with their churches, communities, conferences, unions, and divisions to find the needed funds. Too often, many boards *throw in the towel* to say it cannot work. It is over either for the student to remain at the school or for the school to continue.

As an Adventist educator, I have learned that Adventist schools have closed because of low enrollment, which is linked to lack of funding. Our Adventist schools do not close because of our curriculum. We have an excellent curriculum. I believe the North American Division of Seventh-day Adventists, and I am sure it is the same worldwide, has provided our schools with an excellent curriculum in collaboration with our unions and conferences. Our challenge is not with our curriculum. Our church schools provide a quality education. The real problem continues to be a lack of funding. I mentioned earlier that we have excellent training materials for our boards at the union and division levels for our conferences and schools. Therefore, I have committed to research how to get champions, board members, involved in fundraising to provide the much-needed funds for our schools. I believe every Seventh-day Adventist child deserves or needs a Seventh-day Adventist education, especially at the elementary and secondary levels. Similarly, every Christian child deserves or needs a Christian education, especially at the elementary and secondary levels.

Therefore, I believe that the role of school boards (or even local church boards and other executive boards at the higher levels of the Church) must surpass that of policymakers to include finding funds for our schools. In that vein, I have dedicated a lot of my time researching ways to help school boards with fundraising in our schools. Many schools have partnered with Philanthropic Service for Institutions (PSI), a consulting department from the North American Division that provides training and resources to Adventist schools and other Adventist entities in their philanthropic programs.[2] Recently, Meadow View Junior Academy has included a partnership with a non-profit consulting organization to help with fundraising. I have learned that "boards play a critical role in fund-raising. The most successful organizations know that, and have built a powerful partnership between the board, the executive, and the staff. Unfortunately, some boards resist their responsibility to actively engage in fundraising efforts, or simply don't understand how to be most helpful."[11] I believe this last sentence is true for most Adventist elementary and secondary school boards.

I have found other independent and private elementary and secondary schools to be far more advance in this section than Adventist elementary and secondary schools, and I should say the Adventist schools that I know. Very few Adventist elementary schools are actively involved in fundraising apart from selling citrus, pizza, and the like. Very few are engaged in annual funds, yearly appeal letters to the community where they are located, sending proposals to banks, corporations, and businesses. These fundraising or devel-opment efforts are very common in Adventist colleges and univer-sities but very unfamiliar to most Adventist elementary schools and some Adventist secondary schools. I believe we must find funds for our schools without compromising our beliefs and our mission. By the way, there are many organizations and businesses that will not fund our programs because we are religious schools, but some will and have. Our job is to ask. I strongly believe that recruiting and fundraising for church schools are synonymous to evangelism. In evangelism, you share and invite others to accept Jesus. It is the Holy Spirit who convicts the hearts. It is only the Holy Spirit who brings students and funds to our schools. Our job is to invite and ask.

---

[2] Whom We Serve—Philanthropic Services for Institutions. http:// philanthropicservice.com/whom-we-serve/.

In my research in elementary and secondary school board manuals, I came across a Governing Board Resource for Lutheran Schools[12] where administrators and boards are presented with policies and fundraising samples throughout the resource manual. It was noted that these samples are for schools to consider at their discretion to use for their schools. In chapter 10 which deals with board financial responsibilities, it is noted that "the board is responsible for ensuring that adequate funding is available to accomplish the objectives of the school."[13] It also includes ten characteristics for successfully funded schools[14] as follows:

A shared ministry
- The congregation and school jointly promote and support their ministries.
- The administrator and school staff are available and visible in the church program.
- The pastor is available and visible in the school program.

A united congregational leadership
- The congregation understands and accepts the school and its mission.
- Consistently strong role models support church and school.

A personal mission statement
- The mission statement clearly explains why the school needs financial support.
- The mission statement gives direction.
- Stakeholders know the mission statement.
- The mission statement describes the ministry.

A distinctive education program
- The education program fulfills the goals of the congregation and community.
- The education program offers the community the program it needs.
- The education program provides quality Christian education.

A trained school board
- The board understands school funding is a primary responsibility.
- The board seeks ways to strengthen the funding base.
- The board communicates the financial situation with the congregation and community.

A driven development team
- The development team shows leadership in school funding.
- The development team takes action.
- The development team takes reasonable risks in providing school funding.
- The development team removes burdens from the administrator.

An aggressive marketing plan
- The marketing plan seeks ways to retain current students.
- The marketing plan provides methods for student recruitment.

A strategic financial plan
- The financial plan has a strategy to secure annual cash flow.
- The financial plan is designed for future financial security.

An enlightened administrator
- The administrator realizes financial changes are happening and will continue to happen.
- The administrator prepares personally for change.
- The administrator gathers a funding team to direct the school's financial plan.
- The administrator leads the staff and board through change.

An upfront pastor
- The pastor accepts the school as a ministry.
- The pastor shows a partnership in implementing the mission statement of the school.

- The pastor promotes new ideas in the changing financial times.

The resource manual also provides a historical perspective for Lutheran Schools.[15] It states: "When Lutheran schools were first established in America, congregations usually assumed the full responsibility for all costs. School costs were usually included in the congregational budget."[16] The congregations established the schools to provide a Christian education for the children of their members. The schools were fully supported by the churches and children of the members would pay for books and materials and children of nonmembers were charged tuition. As the enrollment of the children of the churches began to decline and the schools started teaching neighborhood children, it became common to charge tuition. The churches provide a subsidy to help with the needed funds to operate the schools.

The following is worth the attention of church school boards, especially Seventh-day Adventist school boards: "Beginning in the late 1930s and early 1940s, several trends in the Lutheran school movement developed that affected funding practices. Many older, urban congregations became less able to fully support their schools. These congregations, however, recognized their schools as important ministries to the community and therefore were reluctant to close them. Rather than closing the schools, these congregations looked for new sources of income."[17] Since the 1930s and early 1940s, they started looking for other sources of funding while they continue to support their schools through church subsidies. Adventist elementary and secondary schools need to join in these efforts to help make our schools financially successful. Closing schools should not be the solution. The same is true for every Christian church school regardless of its denomination.

The following are the basic sources of income for Lutheran schools: congregational support, tuition and fees, gift income, fundraising, and government-funded programs where applicable. The chapter on funding then concludes with a series of statements as guidelines for their boards to evaluate their school funding program. I believe Adventist elementary and secondary schools and other church schools can benefit from this resource. It is fair to say from the historical perspective of their funding efforts, Adventist school boards can learn from them. In the next section, I will adapt their list for Adventist elementary and secondary school boards to consider, and I encourage church schools from other denominations to do the same. Each school board is asked to discuss the following statements as the current practice of funding the school is evaluated and consider whether the current practices could be improved and implemented. If so, how?

Church support:

- Church support is desirable in every Adventist school. The Adventist school is viewed as a ministry of the whole congregation, not parents only.
- Church members are urged to support the Adventist school and to claim ownership of it as a ministry of the entire church, even as members claim ownership and support the other ministries of the church.
- When planning school budgets, income from the church should be considered first. Conferences are to work with every church to ensure that every church in the conference supports a school based on its income and geographical location.
- Church financial support of the school gives evidence that the church views the school as an authentic and valuable ministry.
- Church members are encouraged to support the ministries of their local churches and the schools to ensure that tuition for every student in the congregation or within the district is fully funded. Each church is to work closely with the school in their area to ensure that adequate funds are provided to maintain excellence in education. Also, to fund a transportation program as needed.
- Churches providing less than full support of the school should provide sufficient support to reflect true "ownership" and a commitment of the congregation that says, "We

value this school." Additionally, churches are to provide in lieu of, budget support, other "in kind" services such as utilities, insurance, building maintenance and other ways that assist the school and give evidence of congregational ownership. Churches should avoid viewing the school as a source of income for the congregation or a burden.

- Churches will annually foster vigorous stewardship programs for all church ministries including the ministry of the school and will thereby seek to maintain or increase church support for the school.

Tuition income and fees:

- Tuition is an appropriate source of income for Adventist schools. Through tuition, parents share in the responsibility of providing a Christian education for their children.
- Tuition rates should be established fairly, based on actual cost-per-student data.
- The tuition collection system should be well-organized and maintained in an efficient manner. Provision should be made for financial assistance to those who are unable to meet their financial responsibility. *No student should be denied enrollment due to the lack of funding.* Each school is to work with the churches within its district and the conference to ensure that adequate funding is provided to cover the tuition of the Seventh-day Adventist Church members. *Each family is to be faithful in returning its tithe and offerings to the church.*
- Practices that violate IRS rulings should be avoided. Tuition may not in any manner be deducted as a contribution to the congregation or school. Tuition may not be stated or implied as a required donation. Contact your conference for additional rulings.
- Guidelines for setting tuition that are fair and appropriately reflect the ministry of the church and school should be established.

- A cost-per-student should be set for all students—members and nonmembers alike.
- When a single tuition rate has been established, the sponsoring churches may provide a full or partial subsidy for its member children who attend the Adventist school or provide a tuition subsidy for unchurched children (not members of a Seventh-day Adventist church within the conference). Churches may choose to provide such support from its worthy student funds.
- All nonmember church families should be expected to pay the full cost of their child's education.
- Other Christian congregations in the community should be encouraged to provide a tuition subsidy for their member children who attend the Adventist school.
- The sponsoring congregation should have a program of financial aid for needy families in addition to its tuition subsidy.
- *No child will be denied enrollment from the school for financial reasons.*

Gift income

- Gift income is a desirable form of revenue particularly when it enables the school to provide special programs and services that are not ordinarily funded by income from congregations, tuition, and fees. Such programs include tuition assistance, equipment and materials, renovation programs, library resources, continuing education of teachers, special equipment, etc.
- Gift income solicitation programs are to be coordinated through the congregation's stewardship board or finance committee.
- Programs of solicitation are to be well-planned and administered, maintaining Christian integrity and avoiding exploitation of any manner.

- Members of the school family (parents, former parents, alumni, friends and relatives of students and members of the congregation) can be encouraged and invited to support the ministry of the school with regular and special gifts.
- Members of the school community (neighbors, businesses, foundations) can be invited to be friends of the school and to provide financial support for it.
- Income from gifts should be estimated and projected conservatively, thereby not distorting the annual budget.
- Gift income, if cultivated carefully and with integrity, can become an important source of income over time.
- Gift income programs should support the principles of Christian stewardship.

Fundraising income

- Discuss the following statements as the current practices of funding the school are evaluated. Consider whether current practices could be improved. If so, how?
- Fundraising is a legitimate source of income when other sources of income have been fully explored and developed.
- Fundraising is viewed as another way that friends of the school can provide additional support.
- Fundraising activities are viewed positively when they are accompanied by Christian fellowship and goodwill, foster educational programs, provide opportunity for sharing and provide adults another opportunity for demonstrating ownership of the school's ministry.
- Fundraising is never viewed as a substitute for sound Christian stewardship.
- Fundraising activities avoid the exploitation of students, parents and friends.
- Fundraising groups work through the established procedures of the congregation and are coordinated by the appropriate congregational committee.

CHAPTER 10

TEACHERS: CHAMPIONS OF EDUCATIONAL AND SPIRITUAL DEDICATION OF THE HEART

The student is not above the teacher, but everyone
who is fully trained will be like their teacher.
                                                    —Luke 6:40

I have always loved my teachers. As a child attending a Seventh-day Adventist school, not only did I look forward seeing them on weekdays at school, I also looked forward seeing them on Sabbath at church. I continue to admire teachers or professors even as an adult. Teachers are very special to me. I am married to one. I love working with teachers. What a privilege to be one of them.

I had never thought of being a teacher, especially after immigrating to the United States in a country where the language was my third language. Being at the seminary was very helpful to me because it gave me the confidence that I could teach. At the seminary, I encountered great professors who taught with accents. They were amazing teachers. They inspired me. When the call came for me to work as a chaplain and Bible teacher, my confidence had already been built to take on the new challenge or opportunity. What a blessing it has been. I continue to teach a class or two even to this day.

In 2006, Dr. Blackmer dedicated a book to Adventist teachers called *Avenues to the Heart—Teachers Who Made a Difference.*[1] He penned, "To the thousands of Adventist teachers who have not only shared their professional expertise with their students through the years, but have shared themselves and the Lord they love and serve. Because of their dedicated service, the Seventh-day Adventist system of education is not only one of the best in the world, it is one that continues to provide educational and spiritual avenues to the heart."[2] So very true. Although teachers are not recognized as much as they should, we, as a society or a Church, would not be where we are without them.

Jesus himself was recognized as a teacher. He was addressed as "a teacher who has come from God."[3] I had the privilege of teaching a course entitled "Teaching Techniques of Jesus"[4] for the lay members in the New Jersey Conference using the syllabus and materials prepared by Dr. John Youngberg (1983). He noted that "N. Anderson (*The Teachings of Jesus*, Downers Grove, IL: InterVarsity Press, 1983) claims that in the Greek Gospels, Christ is respectfully addressed by titles reserved for distinguished teachers over 50 times. Joseph A. Grassi (*The Teacher in the Primitive Church and the Teacher Today*, Santa Clara, CA: University of Santa Clara Press, 1973) says that the term 'teacher' *didaskalos* is used by others referring to Jesus some 48 times in the four gospels, while the Evangelists describe Jesus's activity in terms of *didaskein* some 50 times. The predominance of the teaching ministry of Jesus led C. B. Eavey to say, 'He was often a healer, sometimes a worker of miracles, frequently a preacher, but always a teacher.'"[5]

The pandemic has highlighted the need for teachers in a way that we have never seen nor heard. Teachers are essential workers. They are heroes. Our economy cannot operate without them. I dare to say that our Church cannot operate without them either.

In 1904, a Seventh-day Adventist church in Michigan was looking for a teacher for its church. Haloviak shared the qualifications that were required of that teacher as per Lamson, "We would like a young lady, not too old and yet old enough not to be foolish, who is thoroughly competent to teach any class up to the tenth grade and can teach music, gardening, sewing, hygienic cookery, and perhaps some other line of manual training. We shall expect her to be superintendent of the Sabbath-school, leader of the missionary society, and as often as called upon lead the prayer meeting. The sister that has been our church clerk for a long time desires a change and we presume that at the next election the teacher will be voted in to be church clerk. We hope the teacher will have had the nurse's course so as to teach healthful living to the parents of the children and if any of them are sick, help to take care of them."[6] Wow! This is insane. Teachers continue to be overworked and underappreciated.

As stated by Dr. Tasker, "Committed Adventist teachers who are passionate about God and His children are Adventist education's most valued asset—treasures of inestimable worth."[7] I joined the many who have recognized and valued our educational ministers and evangelists. Adventist teachers like other Christian teachers have responded to the Great Commission to "go and make disciples" and "teaching them to obey everything" Jesus has commanded them. Remember the promise of Jesus when he said, "Surely I am with you always, to the very end of the age."[8] Jesus understood the value, the necessity, and challenges of teaching when he said these words.

Teacher preparation programs throughout the nation have seen a sharp decrease in enrollment. "Across the country, enrollment in teacher-preparation programs has dropped by a third from 2010 to 2018."[9] While I do not have the statistics for Adventist colleges and universities, I am confident they are the same. Recently at a meeting, a school administrator shared that they were unable to get teachers for their schools because education programs in Adventist schools have seen a decrease in enrollment. College students were not getting into education programs because of job insecurity. This reminds me of a conversation that I had with a friend, which I shared earlier in the book, when he heard that I was a pastor and a school principal. He advised me to get into pastoral ministry full-time because the job of the pastor was more secured than that of the teacher.

Teachers as Champions for Church Schools

The first part of this chapter was dedicated to show the importance and contributions of church schoolteachers. They are valued. The Christian Church is blessed with committed Christian teachers. They are part of the Great Commission. They are co-laborers with Jesus, for he himself was a teacher. This section will address teachers as champions for church schools.

Most (58 percent) Adventist elementary and secondary schools are small schools "with only one, two, or three teachers, multi-grade classrooms, and no fulltime principal. Even in schools with four or more teachers, it is common to find multi-grade classrooms."[10] I believe it takes the entire faculty and staff, the individuals who are the most committed to the school, working with the principal, the pastors, board, and community, to make the school successful.

At teacher's in-service, seminars, or meetings, I usually share with the teachers that if there are three teachers and a principal at a school, we should think of the school as having four principals, and at the same time, one principal. I have not read this model anywhere, but I believe it will help our schools thrive. If there is something that needs to be picked up, he or she will not work past it. Each teacher could be as involved as the principal in ensuring the success of the school. Each teacher will be involved in recruiting and in making friends for the school as the principal.

When attending churches, teachers will see themselves as representatives of the schools—which they are. They will develop relationships that will benefit the school. They will market the school as if it were their own business. At the same time, each teacher should never undermine the principal. I believe this spirit of collegiality would benefit our schools greatly. If a parent comes in and the principal is not available, any of the teachers can fill in because everyone is aware of the mission, agenda, challenges, and opportunities of the school. Every teacher in this model will support and contribute to the school program. Everyone works to make the school successful.

While the principal is the spiritual leader of the school,[11] every teacher is a spiritual leader at the school and in the community. I will use the wording in the principal's handbook under spiritual leadership and adapt it to include the teachers as follows: "The personal influence of the teacher as a positive role model to students, colleagues, and parents cannot be underestimated. It is the pervasive influences of the teacher's actions and concerns that inspires others to be drawn to Christ."[12] Church schools need more champions. Church schools need more teachers as champions for their schools. I believe having every teacher behave as a principal will benefit our schools greatly. Principals alone working with a few volunteers will not bring our schools to the level that each school needs to increase its enrollment and fundraising goals. Every teacher must be involved.

One of my pastor's friends shared with us at a devotional that God may have called us as pastors to save us. I believe the same can be said for principals and teachers. I believe *if* every teacher sees himself or herself as a spiritual leader, it will help teachers to view themselves the way that pastors view themselves. This is not a suggestion to create role confusion, but it is to be viewed in the context of the high calling of the teacher and/or the principal. "True missionary work done by teachers who are daily taught of God would bring many souls to a knowledge of the truth as it is in Jesus, and children thus educated will impart to others the light and knowledge received."[13]

The teacher, as a champion to church schools, is a lifelong Christian learner. Such a teacher is a professional Christian educator with all his or her teaching credentials up to date. Such a teacher also presents himself or herself to the community in a professional and Christ-like manner. Such a teacher is also aware of the cultural norms of the Adventist community where he or she serves and with the help of the Holy Spirit, lives above these norms.[14] The teacher who is a champion to church schools continues to learn best practices to integrate faith and learning in every lesson and aspect of school life.

Additionally, the teacher who is a champion to church schools ensures that outdoor and environmental education is implemented in the curriculum not as an event but as a regular practice. As stated by Dr. Gonzalez-Socoloske, "It is our moral obligation to care for nature and that as Seventh-day Adventist educators, it is our responsibility to inform our students about the current state of our planet and the consequences of our choices" (pp. 28, 29).[15] Church schools where teachers and principals are champions will go beyond the call of duty to ensure that children in our churches are given access to our schools. These champions will ensure that the mission of the Church is foremost in educating students.

CHAPTER 11

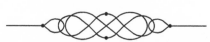

ONE AND THE SAME: PASTORS AND TEACHERS SHOULD WORK TOGETHER

Two are better than one,
because they have a good return for their labor:
If either of them falls down,
one can help the other up.
But pity anyone who falls
and has no one to help them up.
—Ecclesiastes 4:9–10

When I first started to work as a superintendent of schools, I inherited a long-standing tradition of yearly pastors and teachers' meetings. It was a great tradition because it was the only time apart from the end of the year banquet that teachers and pastors would get together under the same roof for a mandatory meeting. I attended every pastor-teacher meeting when I was a principal. I thought they were valuable meetings. We would pray together and listen to presentations on how pastors and teachers should work together. The meetings were planned by the ministerial department and the office of education. At times, I could feel the tension on both sides. It appeared that teachers were never satisfied. They were always asking for more from the pastors. The meetings would also showcase the positive relationships between pastors and teachers. There was a lot of encouragement for pastors' involvement in the schools.

The ministerial and the education departments of the Atlantic Union Conference have published a *Pastors and Teachers Manual* entitled "Together in His Calling."[1] The purpose of the manual is "to provide pastors and teachers with the tools for a team approach to integrating Adventist education into church life as a means of preparing children and youth to be Christ's disciples on this earth and for eternity" (p. 4). The joint message by the ministerial and education leaders continues: "It is the hope that as pastors and teachers, churches and schools, unite their efforts in evangelizing the community in which they are located, a stronger, healthier relationship will result in the winning of many souls for Christ and the finishing of the work on this earth" (p. 4).[2] Historically, the manual cited that "Seventh-day Adventist schools have always existed to serve the major purposes of evangelism and nurture, thus creating a special relationship between the work of the pastor and that of the teacher as the main proponents of Adventist education" (p. 5).[3] Thus, the work of the teachers and the work of the pastors are similar: "evangelism and nurture." Furthermore, it is rooted in the great commission, as stated in Matthew 28:19–20. "Such an imperative implies a collaborative venture of pastor and teacher working together to complete this grand vision" (p. 6).[4] In summary, "without our pastors as leaders in churches and our teachers in the schools, Adventist education would be meaningless" (p. 7).[5] The manual provides practical ways that pastors and teachers can support each other in ministries, which includes a yearly or biyearly joint church/school board, *27 Ways Schools Can Support Their Pastors* (pp. 35, 36) and *25 Ways Pastors Can Support Their School* (pp. 37–39).

Drs. Thayer and Leukert, in their article entitled, "Strengthening Adventist Education—Recommendations for Pastors and Officers,"[6] describe pastors and teachers working together as one as follows: "Whereas the church contains the pulpit for pastors as they minister to their parishioners, the classroom contains the pulpit for teachers as they minister to their students. The 4,000, or more, teachers in the North American Division (NAD) Adventist K–12 educational system, let alone the thousands around the world, are co-laborers with pastors in a common mission. The works of pastors and teachers complement and strengthen each other. In the truest sense, they are a ministry team."[7] Pastors and teachers are co-laborers with God as they co-labor with each other. Teachers should support the churches. Pastors should support the schools. They are one.

As a pastor, I often preach on unity using the prayer of Jesus in John 17:20–23. In verse 21, it reads, "that all of them may be one, Father, just as you are in me and I am in you. May they also be in us so that the world may believe that you have sent me."[8] Praying for unity between pastors and teachers is a prayer that Jesus is ready to answer. It is very much praying according to his will. It is praying using Jesus's own words. Also, as I reflect on praying for unity between pastors and teachers, I am reminded of something that I learned studying small groups at the seminary. I learned that we could answer each other's prayers in our small groups. That is, if someone in the small group is praying for something that we have, we can answer that prayer by providing for that need. With that premise, I dare to say that pastors and teachers can help answer this prayer of Jesus for unity. It looks weird writing this. It is also true between Christians. May Jesus's prayer of unity become a reality in our lives, especially in the lives of pastors and teachers as they work together for and with Jesus.

CHAPTER 12

WHAT EVERY PARENT NEEDS TO KNOW

Train up a child in the way he should go: and
when he is old, he will not depart from it.
—Proverbs 22:6 (KJV)

The Bible tells us that "children are a blessing and a gift from the Lord."[1] Children are gifts to their natural or adopted parents (families) and a blessing and a gift to the Church as a whole. The *Seventh-day Adventist Minister's Handbook* states that the dedication service of a child "emphasizes thanks to God for the miracle of birth, covenants the parents in raising the child in the love of Christ, commits the congregation to provide support for the parents in their responsibility, and dedicates the child to the service of God" (p. 185).[2] The role of parents and the Church is to raise the children of the Church in the ways of the Lord so that not only will they not depart from the way of the Lord,[3] they also will pass it on to their children.

In the introduction of the book *Passing on the Torch*, Dudley quoted Wieting, who made the following observations: "If a society is to continue its existence beyond one generation, the members must transmit what they consider to be necessary knowledge and values. The continuity of a social system by definition requires transmission between generations."[4] Passing on the Christian faith and values should be the priority of every family and church. In Deuteronomy 6, Moses outlined God's provisions to passing on the faith as commented by Smith: "Deuteronomy 6 begins with a reminder that the commands which Moses was about to give them (1) came from the Lord; (2) were intended for observance in the Promised Land; (3) were to be conveyed to future generations."[3]

In Deuteronomy 6:4–9, we read the following: "Hear, O Israel: The Lord our God, the Lord is one. Love the Lord your God with all your heart and with all your soul and with all your strength. These commandments that I give you today are to be on your hearts. Impress them on your children. Talk about them when you sit at home and when you walk along the road, when you lie down and when you get up. Tie them as symbols on your hands and bind them on your foreheads. Write them on the doorframes of your houses and on your gates."[5] God's ways were to be *impressed* on the children 24/7. How can a parent make this a reality? Christian schools give parents the unique avenue to make this command from God a reality. The symbolic act of dedicating a child to God is the expression of the belief that the child is not only the parents' child but God's child (p. 188).[6]

It is the responsibility of the home, church, and school to work together to pass on the faith and Christian values to the children of the Church. Church schools exist to collaborate with parents and churches so that the Christian values and teachings can be *impressed* in the hearts and minds of our children. As I preach on Deuteronomy 6, I share with parents the value of repetition in learning. Weibell outlines the value of repetition in "Principles of Learning: 7 Principles to Guide Personalized, Student-Centered Learning in the Technology-Enhanced, Blended Learning Environment[7] as follows:

> This is perhaps the most intuitive principle of learning, traceable to ancient Egyptian and Chinese education, with records dating back to approximately 4,400 and 3,000 B.C., respectively (Aspinwall, 1912, pp. 1, 3). In ancient

---

[3] J. E. Smith, *The Pentateuch*, 2nd ed. (Joplin, MO: College Press Pub. Co., 1993), 497.

Greece, Aristotle commented on the role of repetition in learning by saying, "it is frequent repetition that produces a natural tendency" (Ross & Aristotle, 1906, p. 113) and "the more frequently two things are experienced together, the more likely it will be that the experience or recall of one will stimulate the recall of the other (p. 35).

As the African proverb states, "It takes a whole village to raise a child."[8] Parents must do their part to ensure that their children receive an education in our church schools at the elementary and secondary levels where the values of the home and church are repeated in the schools. If Christian parents are not able to homeschool their children, Christian elementary and secondary schools are the only viable options. In light of the fact, which I will address later in the next chapter, with the challenge of household incomes, Adventist families who are not able to pay the full tuition should be faithful to the Church in returning to the Lord their tithes and offerings and work collaboratively with their local Adventist school and church to ensure that their children are enrolled in Adventist elementary and secondary schools. The same should be true for other Christian denominations within their own denominations.

During the pandemic, my wife received a call from a parent who had contracted the virus and was behind in her tuition. Early in the summer, she called my wife and me and left a message to say that now that she had gone back to work, she was ready to make payments. This experience brought tears to our eyes. We had prayed for her when she was sick. Now that she was feeling better, she was ready to meet her sacrificial engagement. Another parent called my wife, stating that "now that I have received my stimulus check from the government, I am ready to pay my share." These families were not able to pay the full tuition, but they were committed to keeping their parts of the bargain.

Parents are not alone in raising their children for God. The home, church, and school work together to give access to children so that the words in Isaiah 54:13 can become a reality: "And all thy children shall be taught of the LORD; and great shall be the peace of thy children" (KJV). Furthermore, Dr. Dudley reminded his readers of Joshua 4:5–7, which states that Joshua "said to them, "Go over before the ark of the Lord your God into the middle of the Jordan. Each of you is to take up a stone on his shoulder, according to the number of the tribes of the Israelites, to serve as a sign among you. In the future, when your children ask you, 'What do these stones mean?' tell them that the flow of the Jordan was cut off before the ark of the covenant of the Lord. When it crossed the Jordan, the waters of the Jordan were cut off. These stones are to be a memorial to the people of Israel forever."[9] It is the responsibility of the parents and the churches in collaboration with the schools working with their religious leaders and every level—conferences (state level), unions (regional level), divisions (national level) and the General Conference (global or worldwide) to ensure that their faith is passed on to the next generation and so on. What evangelistic efforts can be more necessary than that of our children?

CHAPTER 13

THE ELEPHANT IN THE ROOM: FINANCING CHURCH SCHOOLS

Give, and it will be given to you. A good measure,
pressed down, shaken together and running
over, will be poured into your lap. For with the
measure you use, it will be measured to you.
                                        —Luke 6:38 (NIV)

If Christians believed that Christian education is a ministry of the Church to the children and youth of their Church, Christians should ensure that it is accessible to each child of the Church regardless of his or her family's financial standing. This statement does not preclude access to non-Christians who are not able to afford the tuition. However, it should be the responsibility of the Church to its children and youth. I began with a general statement with the hope that each denomination would make it its own. As a Seventh-day Adventist, I can say, if Seventh-day Adventists believed that Adventist education is a ministry of the Seventh-day Adventist Church to the children of the Seventh-day Adventist church members, we would ensure that Adventist education is accessible to its members. Adventist elementary and secondary schools should not be a ministry to only those who can afford it.

Each denomination has its own policy on how to spend the funds received from the faithful member of the Church. In this chapter, I will address the current funding formula for elementary and secondary education in the United States as I invite you to address the funding formula at your local church, district, state, regional, and global levels. The current funding formula for elementary and secondary education as cited in the *Working Policy of the North American Division*, V 15 20 Use of Tithe for Education,[1] which I called the elephant in the room, will be addressed in this chapter, with the understanding that policy is not scripture. Therefore, church policies can and should be changed to address the needs of the current times. I will also appeal for systemic change to provide additional funding for our elementary and secondary schools.

A Historical Perspective in Financing Church Schools

In addressing how church schools should be financed, Ellen G. White penned: "Let all share the expense. Let the church see that those who ought to receive its benefits are attending the school. Poor families should be assisted. We cannot call ourselves true missionaries if we neglect those at our very doors who are at the most critical age and who need our aid to secure knowledge and experience that will fit them for the service of God" (p. 217). [2] The demographic profile report of Seventh-day Adventists in North America[3] has demonstrated that most of the families in the churches in North America who send their children to Adventist schools need financial assistance. Many may have chosen to enroll their children in the public school as their only viable option. Here are the facts based on the cited statistics:

- Two in five Seventh-day Adventists in North America live in households with incomes of less than $25,000 a year, a category that includes the working poor as well as those below the poverty line.
- Nearly a third of Adventists (30 percent) are from the lower middle class or households with annual incomes of $25,000 to $49,999.

- A quarter of Adventist families fall into the middle (16 percent) and upper middle (8 percent) segments of the socioeconomic spectrum with annual household incomes of $50,000 to $99,999.
- Just 7 percent of members live in households where the annual income is $100,000 or more.

Based on the statistics above, many families may be qualified for nearly full tuition assistance. Furthermore, Seventh-day Adventist schools must also keep these statistics in mind in their fundraising efforts among Seventh-day Adventist church members. Based on the ABCs of fundraising, a person gives a substantial gift because he or she has the *ability* to give; also because the person's *belief* in your work or organization; finally, because the person has *contact* with your organization or knows someone who knows your organization.[4] I stated before that I believe Adventist school boards *must* play an active role in fundraising. However, they *must* keep in mind the financial constraints of most of the members of the Adventist Church. Every Christian denomination should look at its own demographic profile.

From my research on financing Adventist education, I came across two proposals that I will note. I will analyze in particular the very first proposal as cited by Bert Haloviak (1990), assistant director of Office of Archives and Statistics of the General Conference of Seventh-day Adventists, in the article entitled "Love, Affection, and $1.60 a Month: Early Attempts to Finance Seventh-day Adventist Church Schools."[5]

Historical Perspectives

Bert Haloviak, assistant director of Office of Archives and Statistics of the General Conference of Seventh-day Adventists, in the article entitled "Love, Affection, and $1.60 a Month: Early Attempts to Finance Seventh-day Adventist Church Schools,[6] describes how the wage inequity for Adventist teachers was resolved at the 1899 General Conference Session. In this article, the author quoted a letter written in July 1901 by Percy Magan, the General Conference educational secretary, to Ellen White in which he depicted the plight of teachers, the disparity in wages, as follows: "These church school-teachers have for the most part worked for from $10 to $15 per month and their board. [Licensed ministers at that time received about $30 per month.] They have had no regular boarding place, but have boarded around at the homes of the bredren [sic], staying a week or two in one place, and a week or two in another. You will readily see from this that the salary they have received has been very small indeed. They are the most self-sacrificing workers among us."[7] According to the article, the church's response to the inequity brought equity to church schoolteachers. "As full-fledged denominational workers, they were soon salaried at the rate of licensed ministry."[8] The article also offers a perspective of the root of the problem and how the Church came to find the solution to the problem. I believe we can learn valuable lessons to address the current challenge of financing Adventist elementary and secondary schools today. The solution calls for a systemic change at every level of the church.

Haloviak introduced "Ellen White and the Church Movement"[9] at the very beginning of the article. This is important for us today. The challenge of financing Adventist education is not new to the Adventist Church. When something is meaningful to you, you continue to find and create ways to maintain and sustain it. Ellen White was still alive, which gives us a direct insight to how she counseled the church in financing Adventist education. Haloviak wrote: "When the SDA Church began its church school system, it inherited a financial structure that was in shambles,"[10] due to large debts of its four colleges in the 1890s. Please note that I am not addressing financing Adventist colleges and universities in this book. He continued: "As a new century dawned, Ellen White's son wrote from Australia: 'Mother tells me the time has fully come when our people should withdraw their children from the public schools, and that it is the duty of farmers, mechanic, and business men, to put their minds, their physical ability, and their capital into the work of making our church schools a financial success.'"[11] I must comment on this powerful statement as a church pastor and superintendent of schools.

Adventist church members with children who are not in Adventist schools should withdraw their children from the public schools or any non-Adventist schools and enroll them in Adventist schools. Adventist schools are needed. They are not to be shut down. The financial success of our Adventist schools then (at the time of Ellen White) and today, according to Ellen White, rests on every church member doing its part to support it financially. We still have many farmers, mechanics, and businesspeople in our churches today, and we praise the Lord for them. In addition to these individuals, we call on health-care professionals, government and corporate workers, etc., to financially support our church schools. Every Christian denomination should be able to use the paragraph above in his or her own milieu.

Ellen White did not advise the Seventh-day Adventist church to throw in the towel. Instead, she urged the church to start over with "fresh thinking." "She," according to the same article, "offered a concrete proposal to place the educational system on a firm financial footing."[12] Haloviak noted that "Ellen White donated the proceeds of her forthcoming book about the parables of Jesus and called for the entire church to get involved to help 'relieve the debts of the schools.'"[13] The author quoted the statement from Ellen White that I have used in appealing to churches to contribute to our schools through the years: "Let all share the expense. Let the church see that those who ought to receive its benefits are attending the school. Poor families should be assisted. We cannot call ourselves true missionaries if we neglect those at our very doors who are at the most critical age and who need our aid to secure knowledge and experience that will fit them for the service of God."[14] While I have used this text in sermons and in preparing proposals for church involvement, for the first time during the writing of this book, I felt impressed to research the background of the text to see whether there could be further policy implications not only for local churches but also for conferences, unions, and the General Conference.

I must first begin by stating that I am not a historian. My wife and our son are the historians in our family. I am probably among the few Adventist pastors, perhaps the very few Adventists (if any), who are not too excited about history. For the purpose of this book, I wanted to understand what was going on at the time that Mrs. White wrote the statement that "we cannot call ourselves true missionaries if we neglect those at our very doors who are at the most critical age and who need our aid to secure knowledge and experience that will fit them for the service of God."[15] Was she only addressing church members, or was she addressing church leadership at the time? To be true to the historical context, I decided not to mention all the entities of the church today. However, I can put on my pastor's hat to take the text to our time today to include the other entities of the church where policies are crafted and voted on. These entities are conferences, unions, divisions, and the General Conference. Again, I am not writing as an historian. I am simply trying to see how we can apply the text to our time today to make the necessary changes to ensure that our schools (elementary and secondary schools, for the purpose of this book), God's schools, are financially successful.

The statement under consideration or study is from *Testimonies for the Church*, Volume 6. According to "The Times for Volume 6,"[16] published in 1901, volume 6 was written by Ellen White during her stay in Australia between 1891–1900.[17] This was a time of great missionary explosions of the Adventist Church since J. N. Andrews was sent to Switzerland as the first official missionary in 1874.[18] Official missionary sendoffs, if I may state it this way, were done by the leadership of the Adventist church. Therefore, I propose, the statement under study must have included not only the individual church member but also the church leadership at the time. May I state that she, Ellen White, was also a missionary serving overseas. The church must have believed in sending its best members for this important work. During the time that she wrote that statement, the Seventh-day Adventist missionary work moved rapidly around the globe as noted in the Timeline Summary of the Great Advent Movement[19] below:

- 1876: France and Germany
- 1877: Scandinavia
- 1878: England
- 1886: Russia

- 1887: Africa (Cape Town) and Guyana
- 1888: Hong Kong
- 1889: Turkey and Barbados
- 1890: South Pacific
- 1891: Australia, Mexico, and Central America
- 1892: Finland, Brazil, and Jamaica
- 1893: Malawi, India, Trinidad, Falklands.
- 1894: Chile
- 1896: Japan
- 1897: Belgium and Iceland
- 1898: Peru and Hungary
- 1900: Indonesia (Sumatra) and the Virgin Islands.

During this period of great missionary endeavors, Ellen White, at that time, brought the Church's attention to our church schools that were struggling financially when she wrote: "We cannot call ourselves true missionaries if we neglect those at our very doors who are at the most critical age and who need our aid to secure knowledge and experience that will fit them for the service of God."[20] I believe that the Seventh-day Adventist Church needs to hear these same words at a time when the mission of the Church is focused on un-entered countries, which is a great cause, while our schools are closing, many of our church members are not able to send their children to our schools due to finances. We must find a balance as we evangelize in the twenty-first century.

The reorganization of the Church in 1901 must also be viewed in light of finding solutions to the challenges of financing Adventist church schools in light of the historic vote taken two years prior at the 1899 General Conference Session. The Adventist Church needed to create policies and a structure to bring Adventist school teachers into conferences so that they can be paid not at the discretion of local churches but under the umbrella of conferences. I wish I had paid more attention to my SDA Church history course with the great historian Dr. Knight. Perhaps I would have been able to make a stronger argument. I am thankful for continuous education as a lifelong learner. Let me continue with the article by Haloviak (1990).

He wrote: "Ellen White clearly embraced a corporate approach to educational finance," which she outlined in the early 1900s in the book Testimonies for the Church, Volume 6 as follows: "The subject of education should interest the whole Seventh-day Adventist body. The decisions regarding the character of our schoolwork should not be left wholly to principals and teachers."[21]

Haloviak (1990) commented, "The church was embarking upon a new order. It needed the wisdom of all to devise a sound financial plan."[22] It was at the 1899 General Conference Session that "Irwin Evans, General Conference treasurer, proposed a concept that would become fundamental to the Seventh-day Adventist philosophy of paying its teachers. He suggested that the financial burdens of education 'ought to be divided up and fall equally upon all.'"[23] The author wrote: "Teacher salaries ought to rest upon as secure a foundation as that of the ministry."[24] I must state while I am very proud of the Adventist Church for such an agreement to include the teachers in the payroll of conferences instead of the local churches, the Seventh-day Adventist Church has not created a sustainable model to fund its elementary and secondary schools.

Teachers' salaries are not secured because some of our schools are not financially secured or successful. Every year, many of our schools, especially our small schools, which comprised nearly 60 percent of our elementary and secondary schools,[4] experience major financial challenges. A teacher's contract can be "canceled or renegotiated," according to Union education codes such as the Columbia Union education Code, "because of financial exigency."[25] Since schools' finances are directly linked to the schools' enrollment in any given school year, finding a way to provide greater financial assistance to schools will help reduce the predicament of school closures or the termination of teachers' contracts.

---

[4] Jerome Thayer, Martha Havens, and Elissa Kido, "Small Schools: How Effective Are the Academics?" *The Journal of Adventist Education* February–March 2015): 15–19, https://digitalcommons.andrews.edu/cgi/viewcontent.cgi?article=1011&context=gpc-pubs.

The Elephant in the Room: Use of Tithe for Education

Come now, and let us reason together.
—Isaiah 1:18 (KJV)

In doing research for this book, I came to a syllabus for a course entitled *GCWP101—Introduction to Working Policy* (2012).[26] The course description states the following: "Introduction to Working Policy is an introductory course providing an overview of General Conference Working Policy."[27] The course outline includes the following statement, "Working policy is not Scripture." I approach this section of the book with the outmost respect for every church member and leader at every level of the Church. You might have noticed that I include every church member. My respect is to everyone who is created in the image of God[28] regardless of his or her position in the Church or society. I am not questioning a belief of the Church. I praise the Lord for the way that God has guided our Church in establishing our beliefs as a Seventh-day Adventist Church. I am not writing as a theologian either. I am not. I am a pastor and a teacher. I am most and foremost a Seventh-day Adventist Church member. I also understand more than ever that words matter. So it is not my intention to create a revolution in the Church. No. This is not my purpose. As a pastor and teacher, I praise the Lord for the opportunity to be part of the employees of the Church. I see myself in my humble position as one who has been given a great opportunity. I take this very seriously. I have committed my entire career and life to this.

As I stated at the beginning of this book, my wife and I have been serving in Adventist education since 1998. We have given it our all. We have decided to remain in the same conference by choice. We have always commented that there is work to do where we are, so why leave? We continue to believe the same. We are in a state that does not provide vouchers for private schools. We are in a state with a large percentage of new immigrants in the churches as I have already stated. I have become very involved in marketing and fundraising, even now encouraging schools to send letters to members of the communities where their schools are located. I have been involved in researching, writing, and sending out proposals to businesses, banks, and organizations in addition to annual fund initiatives to our church members, friends, and families. Not only has our family asked others to give, we have also contributed as a family. Several years ago, my wife and I started a scholarship under the name of my parents so that we can give family members in and out of state a reason to contribute to Meadow View Junior Academy. We have done all we can to support Adventist education to make it financially successful. Our churches, even those with high mortgages or rents, have done their best to support the schools for the most part. The only item that I have not addressed until now is what I called, "the elephant in the room."

This pandemic has affected everyone at every level and everywhere in the world. While it did not catch God by surprise, it caught all of us by surprise. Adventist schools, and many other schools (private and public) are very much affected. Based on the statistic shared earlier, Adventist parents are not able to pay the current subsidized tuition. Our schools continue to encourage the families in our schools to be faithful to God in returning their tithes and offerings. Now, I want to raise my voice to ask for additional assistance from tithe for these families and those to come.

When I first received the call to serve as a superintendent of schools, I had a casual conversation about the use of tithe for education with a pastor. I was told that the thinking was since Adventist teachers taught many subjects such as geography, math, physical education, and other subjects that are not Bible-related, the Adventist Church thought teachers could not be paid fully from tithe or at the same level as pastors who are 100 percent involved in preaching the gospel. I thought this thinking was absurd. Out of respect, I composed myself and explained the integration of faith in every subject and in every aspect of school life. I went as far as sharing that teachers serve as counselors, role models, and do many other ministries as pastors. I even stated that as a pastor, I did many activities that may seem not directly related to preaching the gospel, but they are, and so do teachers. It was one of these conversations that needed to stay there.

Several years later, at a year-end meeting of the North American Division (NAD) executive committee, that same policy was discussed concerning supporting our church schools at a higher percentage from tithe. I feel it is acceptable to bring this up because the NAD executive committee meetings are shown live on YouTube. I must state that as an educator, I very much appreciate this type of transparency. Going back to that meeting, based on my recollection, that discussion could not continue because it was not clear whether the policy was a policy that the NAD Executive can change or not without going to the General Conference. If it is a General Conference policy, it needed to be looked at that level. I have not heard any follow-up since. Is it a NAD policy or a General Conference policy? This question is yet to be answered. If it is a General Conference policy, can a division recommend to unions and conferences in its territory to increase the support in tithe usage to its schools? If "policy is not Scripture," should organizations adapt policy based on the needs of the communities or territory they serve? Just wondering.

Well, let's bring out the elephant in the room. In writing this book, I started looking for the policy that limits the support from tithe to our schools. I could not find it in several education codes from different unions. I finally decided to search for a copy of the North American Division and the General Conference working policies. I do not have a copy of the NAD Working Policy. So I searched online and found a 2015–2016 version of the NAD Working Policy.[29] I am using the 2015–2016 version because it was the only version I could find online. I don't think there have been any changes made to the use of tithe for education. According to the NAD Working Policy 2015–2016 V 15 20 Use of Tithe for Education:[30]

> *Use of Tithe in Schools*—"The tithe may be used in support of the various levels of the Church's schools, as follows: a. Elementary Schools—Subsidies of up to 30 percent of the total salaries and allowances of principals and teachers may be granted by conferences from tithe funds. It is believed that this figure should

be a maximum because it represents a reasonable basis on which to evaluate the time devoted by elementary teachers to Bible instruction and spiritual nurture. To increase this percentage would detract from the use of tithe for its primary purpose, the evangelistic ministry. b. Secondary Schools—The equivalent cost of salaries/ benefits for Bible departments, chaplains, guidance counselors, resident hall deans/staff, principals, vice principals, and business managers, plus twenty percent (20%) of instructional employees (excluding contract employees) may be granted by conferences/ missions/unions from tithe funds."[31]

Before commenting on the policy above, I felt the need to do my own research on Ellen White's counsels on the use of tithe. I needed to do so because the premise of the policy stated that "In view of the Ellen G White counsel restricting the use of tithe 'for school purposes,' our system of education must be funded largely from other sources."[32] At Whiteestate.org, I found an excellent resource on the topic of "The History and Use of the Tithe"[33] from Ellen White on the use of tithe; on page 24 of the document, a section called Considerations and Conclusions was provided which states: "Ellen White states that the tithe should be used for 'one purpose—to sustain the ministers,' and that it is to be devoted 'solely to support the ministry of the gospel.' These expressions would seem to indicate that tithe funds should be reserved exclusively to pay the salaries of pastors and evangelists. However, it is evident that Ellen White did not interpret her own writings in such a limited way."

In my view, Ellen White appears to always present well-balanced views based on the issues at hand. The use of tithe is to support the ministry of the gospel, as stated. However, when it comes to "the usage of the tithe in education," she did not provide a formula based on the evaluation of "the time devoted by elementary teachers to Bible instruction and spiritual nurture" as stated in the policy. I wonder, how does one come up with such an evaluation? Students in elementary and secondary schools are ministered to and received spiritual nurture throughout the entire day in school. I am more than certain that this evaluation did not come from Adventist teachers. Adventist schools have always charged a tuition and should continue to do so. However, one cannot use the writing of Ellen White to limit financial assistance to our schools in the form of increasing the percentage of subsidy from tithe. This would not be the accurate interpretation of her writing on the subject. Also, at a time when students, especially at the elementary level, are not able to work to pay for their Adventist education based on governmental laws, her counsel on the use of tithe for education must be taken in context.

There is a quote from Ellen White that is cited under the inappropriate use of tithe for the education of needy students. She provided a counsel that seems to be more applicable to college students than elementary or secondary students. She wrote: "All these things are to be done, as you propose, to help students to obtain an education, but I ask you, Shall we not all act in this matter unselfishly, and create a fund, and keep it to draw upon on such occasions? When you see a young man or a young woman who are promising subjects, advance or loan the sum needed, with the idea that it is a loan, not a gift. It would be better to have it thus. Then when it is returned, it can be used to educate others. But this money is not to be taken from the tithe, but from a separate fund secured for that purpose" (Letter 40, 1897; 1MR 193, 194).

The Adventist Church cannot and should not use Ellen White's writings to limit support to elementary and secondary schools. Conferences may not be able to financially support every teacher at the elementary and secondary levels at the same level of a pastor's salary at 100 percent, but church schoolteachers should be viewed as ministers to our church members' children in the same way that youth pastors are supported by the church through tithes. Not every youth pastor is young, but they minister to the youth. A principal commented that not only do Adventist schools minister to the children of the members of the church, but Adventist schools also minister to their parents who come to the schools for counsels very often.

It is understood that the pastoral ministry (pastors) must be supported at 100 percent from tithe. Based on what I have heard, not officially, it appears that the medical ministry arm of the Adventist Church seems to be doing very well in North America, and hopefully everywhere in the world, on its own. However, the educational ministry, which is another critical component of the ministries of the Adventist Church is and will continue to be in greater need of financial assistance, especially at the elementary and secondary levels, in states and countries where governments do not provide financial assistance or vouchers to schools. The message from Ellen White in the late 1800s and the early 1900s continues to be true to the Adventist Church from the local church to the General Conference: "We cannot call ourselves true missionaries if we neglect those at our very doors who are at the most critical age and who need our aid to secure knowledge and experience that will fit them for the service of God.[34]

Proposals for Financing Adventist Education

As I stated earlier, during my research on financing Adventist education, I came across two proposals: *The Five Percent Solution Making the "Vision" Viable Again* by Thambi Thomas (2012) and the Vyhmeister (2016) proposal. These proposals are described below.

The Five Percent Solution Making the "Vision" Viable Again[35] by Thambi Thomas, associate director for secondary education for the Pacific Union Conference.

To introduce the funding vision, Thomas made the following remarks: "If we truly believe that the work of education and redemption are one" (p. 188), citing a well-known quote from Ellen White (1903) in the book *Education*,[36]

> and that Adventist education is evangelism in action—year round, perhaps it is time to put dollars behind that belief and fund Adventist education as though it were a ministry, an evangelistic outreach of the church! Schools in

the Pacific Union report the baptism of more than five-hundred students each year. Larry K. Downing, an ordained minister of the Adventist Church, expressed the following candid opinion in the Spectrum Blog on July 2, 2008: "The evangelistic programs we spend millions to support are not effective in attracting new members (p. 188)."[37]

I will outline the proposal but will not include the data that he provided for the Pacific Union at each step of the proposal:

Proposal—Step One: Fund Adventist Education, with additional tithe funds

A. Churches will be asked to pay an amount between 2 and 5 percent (percentages are presented in concept/principle, not as rigid numbers) of tithe directly to the conference to help fund K–12 education in that conference.

B. Conferences currently retain 55 to 60 percent of tithe for conference operations. Each conference will be permitted to withhold an additional 5 percent of tithe before tithe is forwarded to the Union Conference in support of K–12 education in that conference.

C. This proposal is suggesting the addition of another 30 percent of "tithe reversion funds" received by local conferences for evangelism which would have provided an additional" funding "to education."[38] His proposal will eliminate subsidies from churches to schools which, he believes, will strengthen relationships between churches and schools. Also, "pastors and principals can forge new relationships driven by the same purpose—the education and salvation of each student in our schools."[39] For the purpose of this book, I will not mention steps 3 and 4 because they deal with operation of school boards, the distinct Adventist identity but not funding.

Conferences should look at the formula proposed by Thomas above to see how much funding would go directly to their elementary and secondary schools to help in their operations. I agree with Thomas's conclusion that "the dream of making the vision viable can become a reality if we who are vested with the powers and authority of leadership would explore all options, all available resources for our children today and for the future of the Adventist church tomorrow."[40] The latter statement has summed up what is needed. A true assessment of the real funding that is needed and find ways to make it happen. It can be done if it is a priority.

The Vyhmeister Proposal of a Possible Solution

It was noted that Ron Vyhmeister, PhD, served as deputy vice-chancellor for financial administration at the Adventist University of Africa while writing the article entitled "Making the Grade."[41] As stated by Vyhmeister,

> the purpose of Adventist education is not to provide employment for members, or merely a protected haven where parents can have their kids in a "safe" environment for a bit longer. Anything and everything we do must be focused on preparing those around us for the Second Advent. If we do not agree on and work toward this goal, our investment may be in vain." Let's agree then on the purpose of Adventist schools. Adventist schools exist to prepare students for the soon return of Jesus. "Working together, homes, schools, and churches cooperate with divine agencies to prepare learners to be good citizens in this world and for eternity.[42]

Vyhmeister proposed a possible solution stating that "considering today's reality, it's time for elementary schools to be attached to the local conference." From further reading the article, it appears that day academy (K–12) would fall under the conference in his possible solution. Secondary schools (boarding schools), he proposed, "should be attached to union conferences."[43] He continued, "Colleges and universities need to be attached to the division."[44] For the purpose of this book dealing with elementary and secondary schools, I will not get into the last proposal, which I must say deserves to be considered so that conferences can have enough funding to support their elementary and secondary (K–12) schools. In addressing the colleges and universities, he penned, "I would not argue that we should close all of our institutions and take them to one location. Rather, I would suggest that the model of the University of Wisconsin System, with its multiple campuses, could be used, where transfer between campuses is seamless.[5] Just imagine the Adventist University of North America, with 13 campuses." Although my doctorate degree is in higher education administration, I have never served at that level. Therefore, I will leave the last proposal for my colleagues at the tertiary level.

Returning to the subject of financing elementary and secondary school, I appeal to conferences to work with the churches and the schools to make it a reality. Under the current policy, elementary and secondary schools (K–12) receive a subsidy from their conferences at up to 30 percent of the elementary teachers' salary. Some conferences, like the New Jersey Conference, have historically contributed more than 30 percent of the teachers' salaries to their schools. Even though these conferences have gone over the policy, the schools continue to struggle due to their demographics and the financial challenges of most of the churches due to in part of high mortgage debts and other factors. A realistic plan based on needs should be developed and implemented to ensure that every Seventh-day Adventist child "at the most critical age and who need our aid to secure knowledge and experience that will fit them for the service of God"[45] would not be neglected.

---

[5] University of Wisconsin System, "UW Colleges' Transfer Guides" (2015), accessed May 15, 2015, https://www.wisconsin.edu/transfer/guides/.

The current funding formula only provides access to our schools to the very few who can pay for the subsidized tuition. Schools that have adopted a policy of giving access to every Seventh-day Adventist child are left on their own at the mercy of some churches that are generous enough to support at their capacity. Such schools are sometimes left with large debts to their conferences. In some instances, principals and school boards are left with no other choice but to reduce teachers or close altogether.

We must pause to ask the question: Are Adventist schools a ministry of the entire Church? Who do the schools belong to in terms of their operations? Historically, Knight commented: "The need to recognize that the health of Adventist education was directly tied to a self-conscious realization of apocalyptic mission."[46] Knight also reminded the Seventh-day Adventist Church that "Adventist education was born in the matrix of a vision of apocalyptic mission, and it has been healthiest when the meaning of the Adventist message and mission is at the forefront of its consciousness."[47] Thus, as a mission-minded Church, we must recognize that we *cannot* "neglect those at our very doors who are at the most critical age and who need our aid to secure knowledge and experience that will fit them for the service of God."[48] We must develop and implement a realistic system using real numbers, based on needs, to support our elementary and secondary Adventist schools.

Chapter 14

A CALL TO ACTION FOR SYSTEMIC CHANGE

*And you will know the truth, and
the truth will set you free.*
—John 8:32 (ESV)

I feel a sense of urgency and responsibility to write this book. Perhaps the title of the book should have been *Help! Church Schools Are Drowning. Do Something!* I am not kidding. This dilemma is not a figment of my imagination. This is my reality which I think might be the reality of many educators, especially the reality of many Adventist elementary and secondary school principals who lead, or shall I say, who carry our schools, sometimes alone. Since I am no longer a principal, perhaps my feelings should have been different.

As a superintendent of schools who is married to a school principal, I am still connected in a way that many others may not be. I know and hear firsthand when the bills are due to the conference, and the funds are not in. I also know of the financial challenges because I am a pastor of a church with several students at an Adventist school in need of financial assistance. The church has done its best to support but can only do so much, especially during this pandemic.

I often tell principals to carry this ministry as if it were their own business, and at the same time, to carry it as if it is not their own. Carry it as if it were their own business so that they can give it all they can. Carry it as if it is not their own business so that they can learn to let go and let God. Sometimes, I wonder if I am able to put into practice my own teaching or advice. *Help! Church schools are drowning! Do something!* But who do we cry out to? As Christians, we have been told to take our burdens to the Lord in prayers.

I have taken the financial burdens of the schools in prayers for many years. I did so when I was at Garden State Academy. Many believed that the academy would not close because the school was a praying school. I learned this very simple but powerful song as a Pathfinder, which resounds in my mind as I write this. "We are His hands to touch the world around us." God's people need to do something to change the conditions around them that need to be changed. Prayer alone will not do. Many prayed to keep Garden State Academy open but did not contribute financially to keep the academy open. I have been told to have faith, and God will provide. It is easier to pray for the schools instead of changing the policies that have kept funding for the schools at minimal. God does provide, but he does so through the faithfulness of his children. It is time to do something to make Adventist elementary and secondary schools accessible to the children of the members of the Church. Each pastor, school and church board, conference administrator, union administrator, division administrator, and the General Conference administrator can do something to change the downfall trajectory of our elementary and secondary schools. The Adventist Church as a whole must provide the financial support that is needed for the successful operation of our elementary and secondary schools.

I repeat, as a Church, we are God's hands and feet. As I continue to pray—and I do believe in prayer—I turn to my church family, local church members, leaders of the local church, leaders at the state (conference), regional (union), national (North American Division), and global (General Conference) levels appealing for systemic change in order to benefit the *needy* students as we sometimes call them. I am crying out on behalf of the needy students, the needy schools. Who would hear and understand? If you have never been needy, it is difficult to understand the needy. I have been there. Maybe I am in there reliving my experience as an elementary school student in Haiti through now the experiences of the many who are attending our schools and not able to remain because of finances. Better yet, for the many who may never be able to join our schools because their families cannot afford it unless we, as a Church, do something.

Help! Church Schools are drowning! Do something! Perhaps this title would have been too bleak. Why write this book now? Let me make it clear that this is not a book to point fingers at any specific individual. It is a book to point to a systemic problem so that we can find a systemic solution. We are a church that is run by policies. Policies are needed to help us operate as a system. However, these policies should not be used as the gospel as if they cannot be changed. They should be re-examined to see whether they are relevant to our time. These policies should not tie our hands to our reality. They can be used to destroy instead of building the body of Christ. They should not blind us to the pain and hurt around us.

Let me restate that I am from Haiti, the poorest country in the Western Hemisphere.[1] I stated this fact to inform my readers to read this book and especially this chapter in context. I can never criticize or speak ill of the poor because I am the poor, and I connect and will always relate to the poor. I associate very well with the poor. So please keep this in mind as you continue to read.

So far, I have shared a lot of personal information, perhaps too personal to some. I came across an article by our General Conference director for Education, Dr. Lisa Beardsley-Hardy, one the brilliant minds of our Church. In the article in which she addressed the state of Seventh-Adventist education, she stated what she called a "well-known quotation" that "without data, you're just another person with an opinion."[2] While this book is filled with my personal opinions and limited experiences, I would like to share, at this time, a dismal statistic. Again, let me set the stage. Please stay with me. I did not set to share this statistic in this book.

Our family continues to carry out the Haitian custom of doing a thorough cleaning at the end of each year to welcome the new year with a clean house. During a most recent end of the year cleaning, we came across an old folder from Garden State Academy. I discovered a list of schools from the New Jersey Conference, my conference. I noticed that 60 percent of the schools that were in operation in the

2003–2004 school year are no longer in existence. This document is less than twenty years later! This is sad. I am screaming out: *Help! Adventist education is drowning! Do something!* As the superintendent of schools for the New Jersey Conference, I have looked at the enrollment history every year and shared opening enrollments to the board of education but have never looked at the number of schools history. We need a systemic change. A Band-Aid will not do. This is not a book to point fingers at any specific individual. There is a real problem.

Schools have closed because of lack of funding, which is associated with low enrollment. We usually blame the leadership of our schools for these problems. However, we need to examine the financial challenges of the families attending our churches. I pray that this dismal reality is not true in other conferences. I have only been in one conference by choice. Perhaps it is providential so that I can bring this to light in a way that very few can. Ignoring it won't make it go away. We must face the reality and come up with systemic changes to address and correct this dilemma.

I signed up for the Trans European Division Newsletter called *TedNews*. In the issue 928, I read an article entitled "Does Poverty Have a Colour?"[3] The article was a synopsis of the final lecture of the Newbold Diversity Centre 2020 presented by Amanda Khozi Mukwashi, the CEO of Christian Aid. The article was inspiring and intriguing and provided a link to the recorded lecture. I listened to the recorded lecture and was amazed at the way the presenter addressed this bold and much needed topic. As noted in the article, "the subtitle added an extra dimension to her subject: 'How the Church can restore dignity, justice and equality for all.' As she surveyed the Church universal and her own Adventist community, her answer to her own question was a resounding 'yes.'"[4] Her closing remarks were well transcribed in the article which states: "The lecture's title question was answered—and more: 'Does poverty have a colour?' Yes, it is black and brown. Is the church in the business of 'restoring dignity, equality and justice to all'? Yes, but it has its blind spots. Our job is to be as clear-sighted as possible about what those failures might be.'" I join my voice to hers to state that while many Adventist elementary and secondary schools are experiencing financial difficulties, those that are serving students in the communities of color are suffering the most. It is time that the Adventist Church establishes policies to correct this. We cannot continue with business as usual.

I pray that God will use this book to help us address these "blind spots." I believe, although Ms. Amanda Khozi Mukwashi, one of the brilliant minds of our Church, did not directly address the decline in enrollment in our Adventist schools, she spoke to all of us, church members, pastors, conference, union, division, and General Conference leaders about the main reason for the decline in enrollment in our schools. The Seventh-day Adventist Church has many church members, mostly black and brown people, who cannot afford to pay the tuition. If we genuinely believe that Adventist education makes a difference in the lives of the children and youth of the Church, we should then do something, all we can, to make it available to all. We cannot call ourselves Christians while we neglect the most vulnerable. Sadly, we have not changed our policies to help the poor who need an Adventist education as any other members of our Church. This issue is a worldwide dilemma.

CHAPTER 15

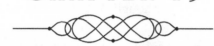

CONCLUSION: I HAVE A DREAM

All to Share the Expense—Let all share the expense. Let the church see that those who ought to receive its benefits are attending the school. Poor families should be assisted. We cannot call ourselves true missionaries if we neglect those at our very doors, who are at the most critical age, and who need our aid to secure knowledge and experience that will fit them for the service of God. The Lord would have painstaking efforts made in the education of our children.[1]

Through the years, I have become a realistic dreamer, if there is such a thing. I am still very hopeful for the future of our elementary and secondary church schools in North America and throughout the world, especially in poor communities. Recently, I heard a scientist shared his views on a country's response to the COVID-19 pandemic. He said it feels like there is a tsunami coming, and instead of looking for shelter, people run to the beach and scream a tsunami is coming and watch. We can't sit and watch. We must do something.

My dream: I have a dream (I pray) that someday every school-age (K–12) Seventh-day Adventist child will have access to our Adventist schools. Parents, churches, conferences, unions, divisions, and the General Conference will make Adventist schools a priority to make Adventist education accessible to our children. It will first begin at the local church level, where pastors will work with the schools (principals, teachers, staff, and boards) to educate the parents and the church of the importance of our children and youth to be in our Adventist schools. Each family will prioritize Adventist education by sacrificing to contribute to the school the maximum amount that the family can contribute for its child or children. The local church in conjunction with the local school and the local conference, union, and division will devise a plan to ensure that the needed funds are secured through financial assistance from tithe, offering, and fundraising for every child who desires to join our elementary and secondary schools. Conferences will change their current financial assistance plan to schools by developing and implementing a realistic plan that is based on real needs.

The discussion of schools' financial needs will be addressed at every committee level from the elders' meeting, church board meeting, school administrators and board meeting, conference administrators, conference executive committee meetings, and so on to include unions, divisions, and the General Conference. The statement at the beginning of this chapter from Ellen White will become a reality with all of us "sharing the expense" in a real way to give access to our Adventist schools to the Adventist elementary and secondary age children in the same manner that we give them access to Sabbath School in the Church. It will become a reality, I believe, if each entity of the Church makes it a priority.

One might say, "But there are not enough dollars to go around." I agree. We have learned a lot from this pandemic. There are many things that we thought were essentials and we have learned that we can do without. Many office spaces are left unoccupied while the ministries of the Church continue during the pandemic. Many businesses are rethinking how to move forward post the pandemic. Shopping malls are rethinking their strategies. We, too, as a church, need to do the same. We have learned that it is essential that children are in schools. They do not learn well without the assistance of an actual teacher. While online instruction may work for some adults, it does not work for young students. The pandemic has taught us that. The Church must rethink how it does the business or ministry of the Church. We need to rethink the way the tithe money is being spent. We must include Adventist elementary and secondary school teachers and principals in the fold of ministers and see their work or ministry, as necessary. Make the changes where needed to provide for our elementary and secondary schools.

Many churches, especially in the new immigrant communities—but not only limited to these communities since some have built or purchased church buildings by adding more debts—are not able to help their schools because they have accumulated too much debt in mortgages. Conferences, unions, and the division in North America must address this issue. They must address it to prevent further accumulation of debts and to give financial relief to these churches. The current policies must be changed because the schools, our children's Adventist education, are neglected in these communities. This issue has created a real challenge where churches must put their mortgages first before helping the schools financially. These must be addressed and corrected.

I appeal to the Seventh-day Adventist Church, my church, to make Seventh-day Adventist education a priority not just in words but in action. I can go on and on. "The Lord would have painstaking efforts made in the education of our children."[2] I know it is a very complex issue. Complex issues must not be left unaddressed. We need to invest in eternity by investing in our schools by giving them what they need to succeed financially using real need assessment, real subsidy, not partial subsidy, where school administrators are struggling to make ends meet. I will end with this: Currently, one of my responsibilities in the New Jersey Conference is to lead the Sabbath School department. I must state that I work with two other great pastors who lead the Spanish speaking and French/Creole speaking churches.

We have nearly one hundred churches and highly dedicated Sabbath School superintendents and teachers in the New Jersey Conference churches. We currently have five schools in our conference with exceptional principals, teachers, and staff—nearly one hundred churches in comparison to the five schools. The churches do not keep me up at night, but the schools do. I learned a definition of fairness as I took a course for my teacher certification. It was a course on special education. The professor told us that fairness is not giving everyone the same thing but to give each person what he or she needs to succeed. She illustrated it as follows: "If I had insulin with me, would I give it to all of you, or would I give it only those of you who need it and in the right doses?" She made her point and summoned us as teachers to always keep that definition in mind when dealing with students. Has the Seventh-day Adventist Church invested a lot in Seventh-day Adventist education? The answer is a definite *yes*! Has the church done enough, or what is needed to address the real needs of Adventist schools? May the Lord help us to answer this question in the affirmative at every level of the Seventh-day Adventist Church. May it be the same for the entire Christian Church for the benefit of the most precious part of the Church, our children, God's precious children!

Sources cited in the article by Dr. Taylor "Joining and Remaining: A Look at the Data on the Role of Adventist Education" (https://jae.adventist.org/2017.3.8).

1. Ellen G. White, *Fundamentals of Christian Education* (Nashville, Tenn.: Southern Publishing, 1923), 436. ^

3. Matthew 3:6, 11; 28:19; Mark 1:5; 16:16; Luke 3:3; Acts 2:38, 41; 8:12–13, 36–38; 13:24; 16:31–33; 18:8. Unless otherwise indicated, all Scripture quotations in this article are taken from the New International Version (NIV). Holy Bible, New International Version®, NIV® Copyright © 1973, 1978, 1984, 2011 by Biblica, Inc.® Used by permission. All rights reserved worldwide. ^

6. Matthew 3:6, 11; 28:19; Mark 1:5; 16:16; Luke 3:3; Acts 2:38, 41; 8:12–13, 36–38; 13:24; 16:31–33; 18:8. Unless otherwise indicated, all Scripture quotations in this article are taken from the New International Version (NIV). Holy Bible, New International Version®, NIV® Copyright © 1973, 1978, 1984, 2011

by Biblica, Inc.® Used by permission. All rights reserved worldwide. ^

7. Kenneth James Epperson, *The Relationship of Seventh-day Adventist School Attendance to Seventh-day Adventist Church Membership in the Southern Union Conference*. EdD dissertation, Loma Linda University, 1990. In this study, 300 family units were randomly selected from the Southern Union Conference of the North American Division, and 210 families responded, representing a return rate of 70 percent. Of the individuals in the study, 40 percent had never attended an Adventist school. Children and youth from Adventist families who were baptized into the Adventist Church had attended an Adventist school for 8.06 years on average, while those children and youth who were never baptized into the Adventist Church had attended Adventist schools for an average of only 2.42 years, yielding a significant relationship (p<0.000) between the number of years in Adventist schools and baptism. The study also indicated that of those who were baptized, 2.6 percent were baptized prior to the age of 8 years old, 63.7 percent were baptized between the ages of 8 and 15, while 14.2 percent were baptized between the ages of 16-23. The 7th grade was the most frequent grade level at which children were baptized, with 61.0 percent of those baptized having been baptized between grades 5 and 8. ^

8. Warren E. Minder, *A Study of the Relationship Between Church-sponsored*

SADRAIL SAINT-ULYSSE, PHD, MDIV

K-12 Education and Church Membership in the Seventh-day Adventist Church. EdD dissertation, Western Michigan University, 1985. In this study, 400 family units were randomly selected from the Lake Union Conference in the North American Division. The study reported a return rate of 71.8 percent and a sampling error of approximately 3.25 percent. The study found a significant relationship (p<.001) between the number of years in grades 1 to 12 that a person attended an Adventist school and whether or not the person was baptized into the Seventh-day Adventist Church. There was also a significant relationship (p<.001) between the church membership of each parent and baptism of the child, as well as between parental active involvement in the church and baptism of the child (p=.0011 for the mother; p=.0191 for the father). Minder also cited results from an earlier study, "A Study of Seventh-day Adventist Church Members," conducted in the Pacific Union Conference in 1962 (N=83,662; 68 percent return rate). That study reported that for young people who had attended all 12 grades at an Adventist school, 97 percent had joined the church, as opposed to 32 percent of the young people from Adventist families who did not attend any Adventist school during elementary and secondary schooling. Further, it was reported that in the group that had received some K-12 schooling in Adventist schools, 57 percent joined the church. ^

13. Roger L. Dudley and V. Bailey Gillespie, Valuegenesis[1]: *Faith in the Balance* (Riverside, Calif.: La Sierra University Press, 1992); Roger L. Dudley and Janet Leigh Kangas, "Valuegenesis[1]: How Does Adventist Education Affect Youth Attitudes?" *The Journal of Adventist Education* 52:4 (April-May 1990): 24-29, 45, 46; Jerome Thayer, "The Impact of Adventist Schools on Students." Paper presented at the 4th Symposium on the Bible and Adventist Scholarship, Riviera Maya, Estado Quintana Roo, Mexico, March 16-22, 2008: http://fae.adventist.org/essays/iv_Thayer_Jerry.pdf. The Valuegenesis[1] survey (1990) received responses from 10,641 Adventist students in Adventist schools and 457 Adventist students in non-Adventist schools in North America. Thayer subsequently analyzed a sub-sample consisting of 2,267 12th grade Adventist students in Adventist schools. The report of a replication of the Valuegenesis[1] survey in the South Pacific Division in 1993 is available at http://circle.adventist.org/files/download/VGCORERE.pdf. A further replication of the Valuegenesis[1] survey was conducted in Puerto Rico in 1995, with reports available at http://digitalcommons.andrews.edu/cgi/viewcontent...and http://digitalcommons.andrews.edu/cgi/viewcontent.cgi?article=1468&context=dissertations. See V. Bailey Gillespie, Michael J. Donahue, Ed Boyatt, and Barry Gane, *Ten Years Later: A Study of Two Generations* (Riverside, Calif.:

La Sierra University Press, 2003); and V. Bailey Gillespie, "Valuegenesis[2]: Adventist Schools Do Make a Difference," *The Journal of Adventist Education* 65:1 (October/November 2002): 12-16. More than 16,000 Adventist students in grades 6 through 12 completed the second Valuegenesis questionnaire. The Valuegenesis[3] survey (2010) received responses from more than 18,000 students in grades 6 through 12 in Adventist schools throughout North America (Bailey Gillespie, "Valuegenesis[3] Update: Research Information Summary," Issues 1-5. Published by the John Hancock Center for Youth and Family Ministry, Riverside, California). ^

14. Roger L. Dudley, "Understanding the Spiritual Development and the Faith Experience of College and University Students on Christian Campuses," *Journal of Research on Christian Education* 8:1 (Spring 1999): 5-28; _____. "Youth Religious Commitment Over Time: A Longitudinal Study of Retention," *Review of Religious Research*, 41:1 (1999): 110-121; _____, "Christian Education and Youth Retention in the SDA Church," *The Journal of Adventist Education* 62:3 (February/March 2000): 8-13; _____, *Why Our Teenagers Leave the Church: Personal Stories From a 10-year Study* (Hagerstown, Md.: Review and Herald, 2000); Jerome Thayer, "The Impact of Adventist Schools on Students" (Unpublished paper, 2008). This paper included a re-analysis of the

Youth Retention Study data. The Youth Retention study (Roger Dudley) began in 1988 with 1,523 baptized Adventist youth ages 15 and 16 in the United States and Canada. These individuals were surveyed each year in order to determine what factors were related to staying or leaving the church. When the study ended 10 years later, 783 (51.4 percent) of the original group, now young adults, completed the survey. Dudley speculated that many of the young people who dropped out of the study were no longer church members. ^

22. Ellen G. White, *Education* (Mountain View, Calif.: Pacific Press, 1903), 30. This redemptive purpose perhaps led Ellen White to urge, "There should be schools established wherever there is a church or company of believers" ("Special Testimony to the Battle Creek Church," [1897], 40).

Notes

Introduction
Time to Get into Good Trouble for Church Schools

1 John Lewis, "Together, You Can Redeem the Soul of Our Nation," *New York Times*, July 30, 2020, https://www.nytimes.com/2020/07/30/opinion/john-lewis-civil-rights-america.html.

2 Ian Lovett, "Catholic Schools Are Losing Students at Record Rates, and Hundreds Are Closing," *Wall Street Journal*, May 10, 2021, https://www.wsj.com/articles/catholic-schools-are-losing-students-at-record-rates-and-hundreds-are-closing-11620651600.

3 "Adventist Education Statistics for 2019 to 2021 School Years," Adventist Education, https://adventisteducation.org/stat.html.

Chapter 1
My Journey in Church Schools

1 Ellen G. White, *Education* (Mountain View, CA: Pacific Press, 1903), https://m.egwwritings.org/en/book/29.100.

Chapter 2
Appealing for Systemic Change

1 Einstein Enigmatic Quote, http://icarus-falling.blogspot.com/2009/06/einstein-enigma.html#:~:text=%22Problems%20cannot%20be%20solved%20by,thinking%20that%20created%20the%20situation.%22.

2 White, *Education* (1952), 30.

3   Michael Holzman, "What Is Systemic Change?" ASCD (1993), http://www.ascd.org/publications/educational-leadership/sept93/vol51/num01/What-Is-Systemic-Change%C2%A2.aspx.

4   Ibid.

5   Mark Connolly, "What Does Systemic Change Mean to You?" Accelerating Systemic Change Network (ASCN), February 1, 2017, https://ascnhighered.org/ASCN/posts/change_you.html#:~:text=All%20systems%20organize%20individual%20pieces,behavior%20of%20the%20entire%20system.

Chapter 3
My Bittersweet Experience

1   Statue of Liberty, https://www.nps.gov/stli/learn/historyculture/colossus.htm.

2   Paul Richardson and Monte Sahlin, "Seventh-day Adventists in North America: A Demographic Profile," Center for Creative Ministry, November 2008, http://circle.adventist.org/files/icm/nadresearch/NADDemographic.pdf.

3   American Immigration Council, "Fact Sheet: Immigration in New Jersey," August 6, 2020, https://www.americanimmigrationcouncil.org/research/immigrants-in-new-jersey.

4   Ibid.

5   Ibid.

Chapter 6
My Service as a Superintendent

1   Shane, Anderson, *How to Kill Adventist Education (and How to Give it a Fighting Chance)* (Hagerstown: Review and Herald Publishing Association, 2009).

2   Ibid.

3   Humberto M. Rasi, "Global Trends in Adventist Education," *Journal of Adventist Education* 55, no. 4 (1993), http://circle.adventist.org/files/jae/en/jae199355040302.pdf.

4   Ibid.

5   "Church Membership Statistics," Adventist Archives, https://www.adventistarchives.org/church-membership.

6   Based on computation from the following data: https://nad-bigtincan.s3-us-west-2.amazonaws.com/about-us/about%20us/statistics/2013-2018%20Report%20Card%20Brochure.pdf and https://documents.adventistarchives.org/Statistics/ASR/ASR2019A.pdf.

Chapter 7
The Big Divide: Pastors and Schools

1 George R. Knight, "2 Ministries/One Mission," *The Journal of Adventist Education* (April–May 2010): 4–9, http://circle.adventist.org/files/jae/en/jae201072040406.pdf.

2 Ibid.

3 Ibid.

4 Ibid.

5 Ibid.

6 Ibid.

7 *Merriam-Webster.com Dictionary*, s.v. "champion," accessed September 15, 2021, https://www.merriam-webster.com/dictionary/champion.

8 Ibid.

9 Ibid.

10 Ephesians 6:10–18, https://www.biblegateway.com/passage/?search=Ephesians%206:10-18&version=NIV.

11 Ibid.

12 Ibid.

13 Newton Hoilette, "The Same Gift: 'And to Some…Pastors and Teachers,'" *The Journal of Adventist Education* (December 1992–January 1993): 4–7, http://circle.adventist.org/files/jae/en/jae199355020404.pdf.

14 Bill Keresoma, "Pastors and Schools—a Dream Team," *The Journal of Adventist Education* (December 2008–January 2009): 27–32, http://circle.adventist.org/files/jae/en/jae200871022706.pdf.

15 Ibid.

16 Ibid.

17 Manual for School Boards at Adventist Schools (2018).

Chapter 8
Churches and Schools: Their Purpose and Goals;
What Every Church and School Need to Know

1 White, *Education* (1952), 5.

2 Jonathan Oey Kuntaraf, "Sabbath School Personal Ministries Department, General Conference of Seventh-day Adventists," *Encyclopedia of Seventh-Day Adventists*, https://encyclopedia.adventist.org/article?id=DB32&highlight=White.

3 Lisa M. Beardsley-Hardy, "State of Adventist Education Report," *The Journal of Adventist Education* (April–June 2017), https://jae.adventist.org/2017.3.3.

4 Ibid.

5 Ibid.

6   George R. Knight, "Education for What? Thoughts on the Purpose and Identity of Adventist Education," *The Journal of Adventist Education* (October–December 2016), https://jae.adventist.org/2017.1.2.

7   Adult Bible Study Guide Education, https://absg.adventist.org/.

8   "About Us—Mission of Adventist Education NAD Education," Adventist Education, https://adventisteducation.org/abt.html.

9   "About Us—Vision of Adventist Education NAD Education," Adventist Education, https://adventisteducation.org/abt.html.

10 K-W-L (Know, Want to Know, Learned), http://ftp.arizonaea.org/tools/k-w-l-know-want-to-know-learned.html#:~:text=Example-,Description,column%20of%20a%20K%2DW%2DL%20chart.

11 Ibid.

12 Howard Hendricks, "What Makes Christian Education Distinct," Christian Bible Studies, July 19, 2006, https://www.christianitytoday.com/biblestudies/articles/churchhomeleadership/060719.html.

13 Ibid.

14 Anderson, *How to kill Adventist Education.*

15 *Merriam-Webster.com Dictionary*, s.v. "religion," accessed September 15, 2021, https://www.merriam-webster.com/dictionary/religion.

16 George R. Knight, *Philosophy and Education: An Introduction in Christian Perspective* (Andrews University Press, 2006).

17 Ibid.

18 George R. Knight, "Why Have Adventist Education," *The Journal of Adventist Education* (Summer 2005): 6–9, https://www.andrews.edu/library/car/cardigital/Periodicals/Journal_of_Adventist_Education/2005/jae200567050604.pdf.

19 Ibid.

20 John Wesley Taylor V, "Joining and Remaining: A Look at the Data on the Role of Adventist Education," *The Journal of Adventist Education* (April–June 2017), https://jae.adventist.org/2017.3.8.

21 Ibid.

22 Ellen G. White, *Testimonies for the Church, Volume 6* (1948), 197.

23 Taylor, "Joining and Remaining."

Chapter 9
School Boards: Perception of Truth Is Everything

1   Hamlet Canosa, *Governing Boards: A Practical Guide to Best Practices & Policies*, Columbia Union Conference, 2008, http://www.columbiaunion.org/sites/default/files/pictures/new_board_manual_07-08l.pdf.

2   *Atlantic Union Conference Office of Education: A Guide for School Board Success.*

3 *Manual for School Boards of Seventh-day Adventist Schools*, North American Division of Seventh-Day Adventists—Office of Education, 2018, https://nad-bigtincan.s3-us-west-2.amazonaws.com/leadership%20resources/administration/handbooks%20%26%20manuals/SchoolBoard_Manual.pdf.

4 *The Journal of Adventist Education–School Boards, Special Issue* (January–March 2019), https://jae.adventist.org/assets/public/issues/en/2019/81/2019-81-1.pdf.

5 *Seventh-day Adventist Church Manual*, 19th ed. (2015), https://www.adventist.org/wp-content/uploads/2019/06/seventh-day-adventist-church-manual_2015_updated.pdf.

6 Ibid.

7 "About School Board and Local Governance," National Schoolboards Association, https://www.nsba.org/About/About-School-Board-and-Local-Governance.

8 *Manual for School Boards of Seventh-day Adventist Schools*, North American Division of Seventh-Day Adventists—Office of Education, 2018, https://nad-bigtincan.s3-us-west-2.amazonaws.com/leadership%20resources/administration/handbooks%20%26%20manuals/SchoolBoard_Manual.pdf.

9 *Seventh-day Adventist Church Manual*, 19th ed. (2015), https://www.adventist.org/wp-content/uploads/2019/06/seventh-day-adventist-church-manual_2015_updated.pdf.

10 The Trustee's Role in Fundraising, file:///C:/Users/saintulysse/Documents/Education/Fundraining%20-%20Trustees%20Role%20-%20NJAIS%202017%20Trustees-DRAFT_11-2-2017.pdf.

11 "Fundraising," BoardSource, https://boardsource.org/fundamental-topics-of-nonprofit-board-service/fundraising/.

12 *Governing Board Resource for Lutheran Schools*, Lutheran Church–Missouri Synod, https://live-luthed.pantheonsite.io/wp-content/uploads/2017/03/LCMS_Governing_Board_Resource_2017_FINAL.pdf.

13 Ibid., 55.

14 Ibid.

15 Ibid.

16 Ibid.

17 Ibid.

Chapter 10
Teachers: Champions of Educational and Spiritual Dedication of the Heart

1 Larry Blackmer, ed., *Avenues to the Heart: Teachers Who Made a Difference* (Nampa, ID: Pacific Press Publishing Association, 2006), http://circle.adventist.org/files/download/06NADE018.pdf.

2 Ibid.

3 John 3:1–2 (NIV).

4 John Youngberg, "ARE 105—Teaching Techniques of Jesus: A Syllabus for the International Institute for Christian Ministries," https://www. sabbathschoolpersonalministries.org/are-05-teaching-techniques-of-jesus.pdf.

5 Ibid.

6 Bert Haloviak, "Love, Affection, and $L60 a Month: Early Attempts to Finance Seventh-day Adventist Church Schools," *The Journal of Adventist Education* (Summer 1990): 6–10, 80–81, http://circle.adventist.org/files/jae/ en/jae199052050605.pdf.

7 Carol Tasker, "Teachers: The People Who Make the Difference in Adventist Education," *The Journal of Adventist Education* 81, no. 3 (2019), https://jae. adventist.org/2019.81.3.1.

8 Matthew 28:16–20 (NIV).

9 Madeline Will, "Enrollment in Teacher-Preparation Programs Is Declining Fast. Here's What the Data Show," Education Week, December 03, 2019, https://www.edweek.org/teaching-learning/enrollment-in-teacher-preparation-programs-is-declining-fast-heres-what-the-data-show/2019/12.

10 Jerome Thayer, Martha Havens, and Elissa Kido, "Small Schools: How Effective Are the Academics?" *The Journal of Adventist Education* (February–March 2015): 15–19, https://digitalcommons.andrews.edu/cgi/viewcontent. cgi?article=1011&context=gpc-pubs.

11 "Spiritual Leadership," Adventist Education, https://adventisteducation.org/ principals-handbook/2leadership.html.

12 Ibid.

13 White, *Testimonies Volume 6*, 217.

14 Romans 14:13–23 (NIV).

15 "Why Nature Matters: Seventh-day Adventist Education in the Anthropocene," https://jae.adventist.org/2019.81.3.6.

Chapter 11
One and the Same: Pastors and Teachers Should Work Together

1 *Atlantic Union Conference Pastors and Teachers Manual: Together in His Calling*, Atlantic Union Conference Ministerial and Education Departments, 2009, http://www.atlantic-union.org/wordpress/wp-content/uploads/2012/08/ pastors_teachers_manual.pdf.

2 Ibid.

3 Ibid.

4 Ibid.

5 Ibid.